Libra

Copyright All rights reserved.
© 2024 Apolo Mantecon
Legal Notice
This book is protected by copyright. Any reproduction, distribution or unauthorized use of the content without the express consent of the author is prohibited.

Author's Notes

Dear readers,

By opening this book, you have embarked on a journey through the constellations of emotions that inhabit the universe of "Libra". Each poem is a reflection of my soul, an attempt to capture the essence of life and its perpetual balance.

"Libra" is not just a zodiac sign, it's a philosophy, a way of looking at the world and finding beauty in its order and chaos. I have written these poems in the hope that they will resonate with your own experiences, serve as a mirror, and show you that you are not alone in your struggles and joys.

This book is the result of years of observation, learning to listen to silence and speak the language of feelings. It is a tribute to those moments of stillness in which, if we pay attention, we can hear the whisper of the stars.

I thank each one of you for bringing these words to life by reading them. Without your gaze, without your heart, these poems would remain in the dark, like stars without a sky.

With love and gratitude,

APOLO

Introduction

In the balance of the stars, under the scale that weighs destinies and souls, "Libra" is born, a collection of poems that captures the essence of a sign that seeks harmony in the chaos of the cosmos. Each verse is a whisper of equity, a cry for justice, and a song to the love that balances the forces of life. Like Libra, this book is a bridge between two worlds: the tangible and the ethereal, the material and the spiritual, the light and the darkness. Through its pages, the reader will embark on a lyrical journey that transcends time and space, inviting us to reflect on the duality inherent in our existence. With "Libra", I invite you to explore the deepest corners of the human heart, where emotions intertwine with the stellar destiny. Prepare to be captivated by the beauty of poetry that flows like the river of life, always in search of the sea of truth and wisdom.

In the clear sky of the mind,
where dreams and muses dance,
verses are born, pure and winged,
like birds that sway in the wind.
With feathers made of fine words,
they soar the skies,
free of chains,
carrying on their wings the rhymes,
that sound in the poet's heart.
Each stanza, a flight without borders,
each rhyme, a beat that rises,
the winged verses, in their sincere dance, weave a network of stars in
the air.
And so, the poet,
with his pen in hand,
gives life to the verses that the soul emanates,
in an eternal flight,
sublime and arcane, the winged verses,
the poetry that flows.

I

In the folds of the ether,
souls dance, whispers of stars,
ancient secrets. William, the visionary,
drew his lines, and
I, a mere apprentice, follow his steps.
What mysteries are hidden behind the stars?
What melodies do they intone in their cosmic dance? Perhaps the
celestial wind carries their answers, or maybe the dreams of the
awakened gods.
The constellations
, like celestial scores, compose
symphonies of light and shadow.
The planets, fleeting notes on the staff, weave stories of love, war and
hope. And so, in the vastness of the ether, we search, our eyes raised
towards the starry vault. We are travelers of the night,
seekers of truths, chasing the wings of ethereal dreams.

II

In times of kings and maidens,
of deeds, crusades, and stars,
a knight at dawn prepares to defend his honor,
his faith, his name.
With sturdy armor and lance,
he rides the already known path,
where dragons lie and princesses
wait to be saved from sorrows.
"Oh, Lord, who art in heaven, guide my sword and my fair fight, that
in your name and glory I venture, and in your sacred love my soul
anchors."
The lady in her tower, pure and beautiful, with eyes like the sea, clear
star, sighs for her beloved knight, who faces evil in true duel.
And upon returning victorious with the dawn,
the people acclaim the hero, the brave, who in the name of his lady
and his kingdom, has brought peace, love, the dream.
Thus in the Middle Ages,
land of legends,
stories are forged that time entrusts,
of honor and courage, of love and faith,
in verses that endure,
that the wind took away,
that time does not undo.

III

In the silence of the ignited night,
where shadows dance to the rhythm of desire,
passion slips, fiery and daring,
like flames that consume fear.
Your lips, two petals in the breeze,
brush mine with infinite sweetness,
and in that kiss, the universe becomes eternal, in an instant of love that throbs.
The moon, witness to our encounter,
illuminates your skin with its silver light,
and in each caress, in each slow sigh,
a story is written that the soul snatches away.
Oh, my beloved, source of my inspiration,
in your arms I find my salvation,
and among sheets of silk and passion,
our bodies intone the most beautiful song.
May the river of our feelings overflow,
may our breaths merge into one,
and may this love, fierce and without regrets,
be the most passionate poem ever written by the wind.

IV

In the city of lights and fleeting shadows,
where time slips through digital fingers,
there is a whisper that cries out for empty spaces,
for moments stolen from the constant noise.
Under the neon sky and extinguished stars,
the essence is sought in tired glances,
and in the pulse of the city that never sleeps,
beats a heart that silently affirms itself.
"Where have the dreams gone?"
asks the wind, as it drags the leaves of discontent, and on every corner,
a nameless poet, writes verses that challenge the horizon.
There is no rhyme that contains the chaos of the mind, nor metric that
measures the persistent longing, only words that flow, free and brave,
in a modern, deep, transparent poem.
Thus, in the era of infinite connections, where each soul seeks its own
orbit, a network of unwritten stories is woven, and in each verse, life
reinvents itself.
In the vastness of the digital cosmos, where souls cross without
touching, there is a cry that resonates in the void, a search for meaning
among avatars.
The streets fill with faceless steps, and on every corner, an artist
without a gallery, paints murals of hope in the air, with brushes loaded
with melancholy.
"What are we but shooting stars?"

asks the voice in the crowd, while eyes get lost in screens, and hands
forget the warmth of skin.
In the labyrinth of connections that trap us,
where each click is an echo in eternity,
stories of love and disconnection are woven,
and secrets are whispered that no one will hear.
There is no poem that captures the complexity,
of this world that spins without stopping,
only verses that try, with humility, to shape what is hard to express.
Thus, in the era of instant information, where each being is a universe
in itself, a long, intense, lived poem is written, a song to life that is
renewed every day.
And in this corner of existence, where you and I meet, let the words
flow, sincere, in a poem that only we understand.
Let the verses unfold like wings,
let the spirit rise beyond the earthly, and let this poem, modern and
deep,
be the reflection of a soul that seeks its truth.

V

In the quiet of a world that awakens,
where the waves kiss the deserted sand,
the echo of a new song is heard,
that slips into the air,
that elevates the soul.
There is no trace of yesterday in this instant, nor shadow of tomorrow
on the horizon, only the now, pure and vibrant, where each beat
counts its own fate.
"Who am I?"
asks the sea breeze, as it plays with the leaves of divine palms, and in
each grain of sand, a small story, becomes a legend, in the dreaming
memory.
There is no poet who does not seek the hidden truth, in the labyrinth
of words that life brings together, only verses that are born,
spontaneous and sincere, in a different poem, in a whole world.
Thus, in the dance of existence, where each step is a sentence, a poem is
written, unique, eternal, a reflection of the being, of the internal fire.
Let the verses unfold like rivers, let them submerge in the soul without
detours, and let this poem, different and true, be the mirror of a
sincere heart.

VI

On the canvas of the sky, the moon draws, with its brush of light, a
path of silver, and under its glow, the night whispers, stories that the
wind relates on its journey. The stars, sentinels of our secrets, blink to

the rhythm of restless hearts, and in the vast darkness, a desire ignites,
like a spark that the universe understands.
"Where are we going?"
asks the wandering soul,
as it seeks its reflection in the shining river,
and in each wave, a dream unfolds, sailing towards horizons where
hope is given.
There is no rhyme that stops the flow of life, nor metric that encloses
its elusive essence, only words that sprout, honest and clear, in a poem
that the night shelters. Thus, in the silence that the moon guards,
where each thought is an odyssey, a poem is written, luminous and
serene,
a song to life that in the darkness becomes full.
Let the verses unfold like waves, let them submerge in the soul without
delay, and let this poem, born of the night, be the refuge of a heart that
strips itself.

VII

In the garden of time,
where moments bloom,
each petal is a memory,
each scent is a before,
and in the whisper of the leaves,
ancient secrets are told,
of loves that were eternal,
of dreams that remain alive.
"What is life but a canvas?"
asks the painter,
as he traces with colors the silhouette of love,
and in each brushstroke, an emotion overflows,
creating in the canvas a world where passion is crowned.
The statues in the park,
witnesses to a thousand stories, observe in silence the glories and the
memories,
and in the dance of the shadows, as the evening falls, the beauty of
what the heart guards is revealed.
There is no verse that does not long to capture the pure essence,
of this universe that envelops us, of this secure nature, only words that
intertwine,
strong and deep, in a poem that is born from the soul, from its fertile
roots.

Thus, in the garden of time, where each flower is a poem, where each path leads to the supreme truth, a story is written, delicate and strong, a song to life, to luck, to death.
Let the verses unfold like branches in the wind, let them nest in the soul without a single regret, and let this poem, born in the garden of being, be the refuge of a heart that seeks to bloom.

VIII

On the canvas of a dream that unfolds, where the colors of dawn
intermingle, there is a voice that sings to life, that in each note, hope
nests.
"What is love but a flight?"
asks the wind, as it caresses the flowers in its slow movement, and in
each petal, a desire awakens, a longing for union that the deserted
distance. The mountains, guardians of ancient promises, stand firm,
majestic and thick, and at their peak, the sun greets the day, painting
gold the melancholy.
There is no poetry that does not aspire to be eternal, to capture beauty
in its tenderest form, only verses that flow, pure and alive, in a poem
that celebrates the captive senses.
Thus, on the canvas of a new dawn, where each stroke is a rebirth, a
poem is written, fresh and sincere, a tribute to life, to first love. Let the
words unfold like birds, that in the sky of the soul their routes are
serious.

IX

In the deepest corner of the mind, where thoughts are latent seeds,
ideas sprout, fresh and bright, like stars that illuminate the moments
. "What is being but a mighty river?"
the soul questions, as it flows among the rocks of calm, and in each
whirlpool, a truth is revealed, knowledge that shines in the current.
The trees of the forest, wise and ancient, whisper stories in extinct
languages, and in the murmur of the leaves, given to the wind, the
wisdom of past ages is discovered.
There is no poem that does not desire to embrace the infinite, to
capture the mystery in its exquisite flight, only verses that unfold, bold
and free, in a poem that is born from the fire that vibrates.
Thus, in the universe of imagination, where each idea is a new creation,
a poem is written, vibrant and diverse, a reflection of the cosmos, of
destiny, of verse.
Let the words unfold like wings in the sky, that in the heart of the
reader they find their longing, and let this poem, born of the creative
spark, be the song of a spirit that is kindled in poetry.

X

In the quiet of a golden dawn, where the sun awakens with a winged yawn, the day unfolds, slow and calm, and in its light, a new dream is sown.
"What is hope but a distant lighthouse?"
the horizon questions, as it paints the mountain with colors, and in each ray of sun, a promise is forged, a path of light that approaches the heart.
The rivers, mirrors of the sky on earth, reflect the clouds that enclose peace, and in the murmur of the water, clear and serene, the song of full life is heard. There is no poetry that does not seek to reach immensity, of this world full of beauty and truth, only verses that are written, with love and faith, in a poem that embraces life, that satisfies the soul. Thus, on the canvas of a day that begins, where each color is a reward, a poem is written, luminous and warm, a tribute to the sun, to love, to courage. Let the words unfold like rays of light, that illuminate the soul without any cross, and let this poem, born of the dawn, be the refuge of a heart that seeks to be reborn.

XI

Under the mantle of stars that the night unfolds, where each light is a
whisper from the celestial vault, a story of silences and lights is woven,
a tale that the universe in its infinity confesses.
"What is time but a flowing river?"
eternity asks, while the constellations draw maps of destinies, and in
each shooting star, a desire ignites, a hope that in the darkness finds
paths.
The trees whisper in tongues of wind and leaf, telling legends of deep
roots and tall crowns, and in the song of nature, a melody is woven, a
symphony of life that is exalted in silence.
There is no poetry that does not try to capture the sigh of the world,
the essence of what we are, of what we will be, only verses that are
thrown, brave and deep, in a poem that seeks its temple in the night.
Thus, under the mantle of stars, in the quiet of the cosmos, where each
light is a verse, each shadow is a poem, an ode to immensity is written,
to the mystery, a song to the universe, to life, to the diadem.
Let the verses unfold like expanding galaxies,
that in the soul of the reader they resonate with passion, and let this
poem, born of the starry night,
be the embrace of a sky that has landed on earth.

XII

In the whisper of a sunset that fades, where the sky is tinged with
brushstrokes of fire, the promise of a day that is reborn is found, and in
its goodbye, the hope of a new game.
"What is life but an endless cycle?"
the twilight asks, as the clouds say goodbye with a last glow, and in
each shade of light, a story closes, a chapter that ends, a memory that
remains beautiful.
The birds, messengers of air and time, trace routes in the sky with their
dancing wings, and in the ballet of their flight, a dance is composed, a
choreography of farewells and routines.
There is no poem that does not wish to capture the moment,
the magic of what happens, of what stays ahead, only verses that are
written, with nostalgia and with the present, in a poem that embraces
the now, that smiles at the future.
Thus, on the canvas of a sunset that is extinguished, where each tone is
a sigh, each shadow is a link, a poem is written, soft and persistent, a
tribute to the day that leaves, to the one that comes, to its embrace.
Let the words unfold like leaves in the wind, that in the soul of the
reader they find their moment, and let this poem, born of the sunset,
be the refuge of a heart that seeks to understand.

XIII

In the silence of a whispering forest,
where the leaves tell stories to the wind,
a refuge of peace and murmurs is discovered,
a sanctuary where time stops, slow.
"What is knowledge but a path?"
the wise man asks, as he walks among centennial trees, and in each
step, a lesson is revealed,
a learning that in the earth is sown.
The rivers,
masters of flow and change, sing melodies of clear and pure waters,
and in the reflection of their course, a truth appears, a certainty that in
the current endures.
There is no poetry that does not long to be a river, to be a forest, to be
wind, to be shelter, only verses that intertwine, with calm and vigor, in
a poem that is born from the soul, that for the spirit is shelter.
Thus, in the silence of a listening forest, where each tree is a verse, each
shadow is a poem, an ode is written to introspection, to the search, a
song to nature, to life, to greatness.
Let the verses unfold like roots in the earth, that in the soul of the
reader they find their dwelling, and let this poem, born of stillness, be
the embrace of a forest that has landed on earth.

In the dance of life, where each step is an art, where the rhythm of the world beats in every part, the melody of existence is discovered, and in its beat, the essence of resistance.

"What is art but the voice of the soul?" the painter asks, as his brush brings life to color, and in each stroke, a passion is unleashed, a fire that on the canvas of time is portrayed. The poets, architects of dreams and words, build bridges between worlds, between looks, and in the verse of their pen, a truth is written, a declaration of love that survives on paper. There is no poetry that does not dream of being eternal, to be a refuge, to be light in the cave, only verses that intertwine, with strength and tenderness, in a poem that is born from pure inspiration.

Thus, in the dance of life, where each turn is a poem, where each jump is a challenge, a diadem, a story is written, vibrant and sincere, a song to existence, to passion, to waiting.

Let the verses unfold like wings in the wind, that in the heart of the reader they find their accent, and let this poem, born of the dance and the moment, be the refuge of a spirit in constant movement.

On the shore of a murmuring river, where the water caresses the stone, life unfolds, serene and secure, and in its course, a reflection of pure nature.

"What is the reflection but a dialogue with the soul?" the mirror asks, as it captures the image of the sky and the old man, and in each wave, a memory stirs, a memory that in the water slides and throbs.

The birds, composers of the symphony of the air, sing songs of freedom, without disdain, and in the concert of their trills, a peace nests, a tranquility that in the forest is invited. There is no poetry that does not aspire to be a song, to be a river, to be a breeze, to be passion, only verses that intertwine, with rhythm and reason, in a poem that is born from the heart, that gives vision to the spirit.

Thus, on the shore of a river that tells stories, where each stone is a verse, each plant is glory, an ode to flowing, to being, to being, a song to water, to life, to loving.
Let the verses unfold like the river on its way, that in the soul of the reader they find their destiny, and let this poem, born of the current and the feeling, be the refuge of a heart that seeks to live.

XIV

In the quiet of the night, when the world sleeps, and the stars twinkle like beacons in the vastness, there is a whisper that pierces the silence, a voice that sings to the moon, to eternity.
"What is desire but a fire that burns?"
passion asks, as it ignites souls with its fiery dance, and in each spark, a story ignites, a dream that in the darkness becomes present. The lovers, navigators of seas of sheets, explore horizons of skin and sighs, and in the meeting of their bodies, a promise is sealed.
A pact of love that is inscribed in time. There is no poetry that does not seek to be eternal, to be memory, to be echo, to be flame that winters, only verses that intertwine, with passion and calm, in a poem that is born from the soul, that awakens the heart. Thus, in the quiet of the night, where each star is a verse,
where each silence is a poem, a confession, a story of love, of desire, of fusion, a song to passion, to life, to the song.
Let the verses unfold like waves in the ocean, that in the soul of the reader they find their port, and let this poem, born of the night and desire, be the refuge of a heart that seeks comfort.

XV

In the vastness of the sky, where the clouds wander, and the blue
extends like an endless canvas, there is a moment of quiet, of sacred
reflection, where the being is found, and the journey begins there.
"What is contemplation but a bridge to the soul?"
the thinker asks, as he immerses himself in the sea of his own mind,
and in each wave of thought, a revelation unfolds, an understanding
that is felt in the depth.
The trees, pillars of the earth, whisper in the wind, stories of roots and
leaves, of cycles and time, and in the whisper of nature, a calm is
breathed, a serenity that in the forest is consecrated and seen.
There is no poetry that does not try to be a reflection, to be an echo of
the internal, to be light in the mirror, only verses that intertwine, with
quietude and mystery, in a poem that is born from introspection, from
silence.
Thus, in the vastness of the sky, where each cloud is a thought, where
each ray of sun is an idea, an inspiration, an ode is written to
contemplation, to discovery, a song to the sky, to life, to meditation.
Let the verses unfold like the wind among the branches, that in the
soul of the reader they find their echo, their home, and let this poem,
born of contemplation and calm, be the refuge of a spirit that seeks to
look beyond.

XVI

In the quiet of a world that awakens, where the sun greets with its warm embrace, life unfolds, slow and alert, and in its light, a new dream is welcomed.
"What is dawn but a rebirth?"
the day asks, as it tints the sky with hues of hope, and in each ray of light, a promise nests, a beginning that is launched on the horizon. The birds, heralds of dawn, sing in chorus, announcing the arrival of a new time, and in the concert of their song, a joy is breathed, a symphony of life that rises in the air.
There is no poetry that does not seek to be breath, to be inspiration, to be light in the moment, only verses that intertwine, with illusion and fervor, in a poem that is born from the dawn, that gives warmth to the heart.
Thus, in the quiet of a world that is illuminated, where each color is a verse, each shadow is a poem, an ode is written to the new day, to life, a song to the sun, to hope.
Let the verses unfold like the sun on its way, that in the soul of the reader they find their destiny, and let this poem, born of the dawn and the feeling, be the refuge of a heart that seeks to live.

XVII

On the canvas of dawn,
where the sky dresses up,
with shades of pink and orange that the sun scatters, the world
awakens,
with a yawn of light, and in its embrace,
life begins its walk, its cross.
"What is awakening but a promise?"
the dawn asks,
as it draws back
the curtains of the night,
without fail, and in each flash,
a hope is renewed, a dream
that rises on the horizon.
The birds, orchestra of the day,
tune their songs,
prelude to a concert
that awakens the charms,
and in the melody of dawn,
a peace is installed, a serenity
that is given away in the air.
There is no poetry
that does not aspire to be light,
to be a guide, to be breath in the struggle,
only verses that intertwine,
with delicacy and vigor

, in a poem that is born from the dawn,
that gives relief to the heart.
Thus, on the canvas of dawn,
where each color is a verse,
where each ray of sun is a poem,
a universe, an ode is written to the new day,
to the illusion, a song to the sun, to life, to passion.
Let the verses unfold like the sun in its ascent,
that in the soul of the reader they find their rest,
and let this poem, born of light and desire,
be the refuge of a heart that seeks its longing.

XVIII

In the sway of the waves, where the sea kisses the sand, and the foam
draws patterns of salt and chimera, the song of the ocean is heard,
deep and ancestral, and in its embrace, the earth and water unite in a
ritual.
"What is the tide but a dance of the moon?"
the beach wonders, while welcoming the caresses of the water, without
falter, and in each wave that arrives,
a story is told, a tale of journeys, of encounters, of life that presents
itself.
The seagulls, acrobats of the wind, soar in the sky, drawing figures of
freedom, without longing, and on the blue canvas, a dance is traced, a
choreography of wings that the horizon embraces.
There is no poetry that does not wish to be a wave, to be sea breeze, to
be a comforting song, only verses that intertwine, with the rhythm of
the tide, in a poem that is born from the sea, that gives itself to the
beach.
Thus, in the sway of the waves, where each foam is a verse, where each
grain of sand is a poem, a universe, an ode to the sea is written, to its
immensity, a song to the waves, to life, to eternity.
May the verses unfold like the waves at their crest, may they find their
celebration in the soul of the reader, and may this poem, born from
the sea and its song, be the refuge of a heart that seeks its charm.

XIX

In the whisper of the wind, where the leaves dance, and autumn paints
the world with its palette of hopes, the melody of a time that renews
itself is heard, and in its cycle, life weaves its fabric, its test.
"What is change but a door that opens?"
the forest wonders, while it dresses in ochres, yellows and touches, and
in each leaf that falls, a story is released, a memory that is sown in the
earth, that waits. The animals, guardians of change, prepare, for the
winter that arrives, that clarifies everything, and in the preparation of
their refuge, wisdom is shown, a lesson of adaptation that is gestated in
nature.
There is no poetry that does not wish to be change, to be
transformation, to be step, to be rank, only verses that intertwine, with
the rhythm of the seasons, in a poem that is born from autumn, that
brings emotions to hearts. Thus, in the whisper of the wind, where
each leaf is a verse, where each branch is a poem, a universe, an ode to
change is written, to transition, a song to the leaves, to life, to vision.
May the verses unfold like leaves in the wind, may they find their
accent in the soul of the reader, and may this poem, born from autumn
and its song, be the refuge of a heart that seeks its charm.

XX

In the abyss of the cosmos,
where galaxies spin, and stars narrate epics of light and mystery, the
universe unfolds,
immense and eternal, and in its vastness,
life is discovered, admired.
"What is existence but a stellar journey?"
the night wonders, while the firmament is adorned with celestial
jewels, and in each constellation, a legend is forged, a myth that is
inscribed in space, that defies endings. The comets, messengers of the
void, cross the sky, leaving behind trails of ice and fire, and on the
black canvas, a story is painted, an odyssey of particles that time does
not extinguish.
There is no poetry that does not long to be a universe, to be
exploration, to be discovery, to be verse.
only words that intertwine,
with the gravity of the stars,
in a poem that is born from the impression,
that gives ties to hearts.
Thus, in the abyss of the cosmos,
where each star is a poem, where each black hole is a mystery, an ode
to greatness is written, to immensity, a song to creation, to eternity.
May the verses unfold like supernovas in explosion,
may they find their dimension
in the soul of the reader,
and may this poem,

born from the impression and from the wonder,
  be the refuge of a spirit that seeks its shadow.

XXI

In the whisper of the breeze, where thoughts fly, and the sky extends like a mantle of possibilities, imagination unfolds, without limits or borders, and in its freedom, creativity flourishes, it is unleashed.
"What is inspiration but a sigh of the soul?"
the poet wonders, while words spring up like springs from the mind, and in each verse, a vision crystallizes, a flash of genius that becomes present on paper.
The muses, weavers of dreams and art, thread stories on the loom of fantasy, and in the fabric of their work, a beauty is revealed, a work of ingenuity that in inspiration is trusted.
There is no poetry that does not seek to be flight, to be journey, to be discovery, to be sky, only verses that intertwine, with the grace of the clouds, in a poem that is born from the breath, that rises to hearts.
Thus, in the whisper of the breeze, where each thought is a verse, where each idea is a poem, a universe, an ode to the muse, to imagination is written, a song to creativity, to life, to passion.
May the verses unfold like leaves in the wind, may they find their accent in the soul of the reader, and may this poem, born from the breeze and the moment, be the refuge of a spirit in constant motion.

XXII

In the silence of the night,
when the stars converse,
and the moon listens attentively,
guardian of confessions,
a mantle of mystery unfolds,
woven with threads of silver,
and in its embrace, dreams slide, intertwine.
"What is mystery but a door to infinity?"
the universe wonders,
while it unfolds its secrets in a dance of lights and shadows, and in
each flash, a curiosity awakens, an enigma that in the immensity of
space is embroidered.

The comets, travelers of the void, plow through the darkness, leaving
behind traces of stardust and stories, and on the canvas of the night,
an adventure is drawn, an odyssey of time and space that memory
treasures.
There is no poetry that does not wish to be discovery, to be
exploration, to be an answer to the wind, only verses that intertwine,
with the grace of the dawn, in a poem that is born from silence, that
flourishes in hearts.
Thus, in the silence of the night, where each star is a verse, where each
whisper is a poem, a universe, an ode to mystery is written, to
contemplation, a song to the night, to life, to imagination.

May the verses unfold like constellations in the sky, may they find their longing in the soul of the reader, and may this poem, born from the night and its charm, be the refuge of a spirit that seeks its song.

La curiosidad

In the laboratory of life,
where ideas bubble, and knowledge is distilled like an elixir of the
mind, curiosity unfolds, restless and brilliant, and in its search,
discovery presents itself, imposing.
"What is curiosity but a divine spark?"
the sage wonders, while mixing the ingredients of the question and the
answer, and in each experiment, an understanding is reached, a finding
that in the book of knowledge is noted, is strengthened.
The inventors, alchemists of the possible, forge in their workshop,
creations that transform the world, that defy yesterday, and in the
forge of their ingenuity, an innovation is shaped, a solution that in the
history of humanity is threaded.
There is no poetry that does not wish to be discovery, to be revelation,
to be light in thought, only verses that intertwine, with the precision
of science, in a poem that is born from curiosity, that gives license to
reason.
Thus, in the laboratory of life, where each idea is a verse, where each
solution is a poem, a universe, an ode to ingenuity is written, to
exploration, a song to curiosity, to life, to innovation.
May the verses unfold like theories in the mind, may they find their
seed in the soul of the reader, and may this poem, born from curiosity
and knowledge, be the refuge of a spirit that seeks to understand.

The night sky

On the canvas of the night sky, the stars dance,
bright and distant.
The murmur of the sea accompanies their waltz, while the moon, in its
splendor, guides them.
Under the celestial dome, dreams intertwine, stories of lost loves, of
forgotten heroes.
Each star, a story; each constellation, a poem, written in eternity, for
those who wish to look.
The nocturnal breeze whispers ancient secrets, of mystical lands and
legendary creatures.
The universe, a tapestry of endless mysteries, invites us to explore, to
dream, to live.
Thus, in the quiet of the night,
I find myself, contemplating the infinite, feeling its embrace.
And at this moment, under the immense firmament,
I am a poet, I am a dreamer, I am part of everything.

The Infinite

Beyond the horizon,
where the sky kisses the sea, the infinite extends,
vast and without end.
A realm of possibilities, an unpainted canvas, where each star is a wish,
waiting to shine.
The infinite, a mystery that calls us to explore, a journey without
destination, an eternity to dream.

It is the echo of creation, the voice of the universe, that in its profound
silence, reveals its verse to us.
In the embrace of the infinite, we are stardust, travelers of time,
seeking beautiful answers.
It is the dance of life, the endless cycle, where everything transforms,
and everything returns to its origin.
Thus, in the contemplation of immensity, we feel freedom, the pure
truth. The infinite teaches us that in its vastness, every moment is
unique, and every dream, reality.

XXIII

Under the celestial mantle of a golden dream,
where the sun stretches its silver rays,
the earth awakens in a song of light,
and life dresses in its best suit of blue.
In the blooming valley,
the river meanders,
with its crystal waters that the breeze combs
, and in its course, the stones tell stories,
of ancient travelers and their memories.
The trees whisper in the enchanted forest, with leaves that dance to the
rhythm of the beloved wind, and among their branches, a choir of
birds sings, melodies that enchant the soul of the world.
On the top of the mountain, the horizon extends, a canvas of colors
that kindles the heart, and the traveler, on its summit, admires in awe,
the work of art that the universe has gifted.
The night arrives with its starry mantle, and the moon, on its throne,
has been crowned, queen of darkness, guide of dreamers, who in its
light find their greatest loves.
And so, in each verse that my pen writes, a story is woven that lives in
time, a long poem of infinite beauty, that always dwells in the pages of
the soul.

XXIV

In the realm of the verb where dawn is born, where time stands still
and silence speaks, there I weave with words a tapestry of dreams,
where each stanza is a world, and the worlds, eternal.
With the ink of the stars and the paper of the sky, I write verses that
embrace the entire universe, each letter, a sigh from the mother earth,
each word, a heartbeat that burns.
I speak of loves that never wither, of passions that in the soul ignite
and throb, of the hope that shines in the darkness, like a lighthouse
guiding the lost ship. I sing to life with its sweet mystery, to the dance
of the rain, to the fire of summer, to the flight of the hummingbird, to
the lone wolf, to the strength of the river, to the spirit of the
neighborhood.
And in this poem, a tribute to creation, to each being, to each idea, to
each song, that in the great concert of existence, plays its part with
fervor and essence.
Thus, the best poet, in humble offering, leaves in each verse a light that
extends, to illuminate paths, to touch hearts, and to unite in a single
song, infinite emotions.
In the vastness of the cosmos, between lights and shadows, where
dreams are forged and reality astonishes, there a poem is born, like a
river that flows, with words that dance and build in the soul.
It is a song to the earth, with its seas and rivers, to the mountains that
guard ancient challenges, to the valleys that sleep under the infinite
sky, and to the flowers that bloom with their blessed color.

I speak of the night, with its veil of mysteries, of the moon that observes the serious lovers, of the silence that listens to the confession of the wind, and of the stars that guard time.
I sing to passion, that flame that does not cease, that weighs in the chest of man and woman, that unites them in a dance of eternal harmony, and that paints the poetry of the day red.

XXV

In the twilight of a hidden love, where desire dresses in mourning, two souls meet in secret, united by a discreet feeling.
He, of the light, she, of the shadow, in a world that their union astonishes, lovers forbidden by destiny, with a love so strong and genuine.
They love each other in silence, without words, in a language that the heart carves, their gazes cross and say it all, in a parallel universe, apart from the mud.
Their hands brush with fear and longing, each caress is a flight to heaven, but time is cruel, they cannot stay, only in dreams do they truly love each other.
He, like the sun that faces the sunset, she, like the moon that is counted in the night, they will never be able to merge into an eternal eclipse, their love is a fire that burns in the winter.
But in the depth of their forbidden passion, they find comfort for their painful life, they know that even though the world separates them, on the spiritual plane, they will always love each other without repair.

And so, between whispers and hidden tears, they live their love in lost dimensions, two souls that love each other with divine strength, even though their destiny denies them the rhyme.
In the quiet of the night, their love intensifies, each furtive encounter, the passion justifies, in the secret garden of their twin souls, desires bloom, the most beautiful promises.

Although the world judges them, their love is immortal, beyond the physical, in the spiritual, like two stars spinning in the same orbit, although separated, their light keeps shining.

In each stolen embrace, in each hidden kiss, a universe is revealed that had remained, hidden in the sigh of captive lovers, in the gaze they share, intense and alive.

And when the dawn announces the new day, with tears in their eyes, they say goodbye with poetry, 'It doesn't matter the distance, nor the cruel barrier, our love is eternal, like spring.'

This is how lovers live, with hope in their hands, that one day they will break all the arcane, and their forbidden love, will finally be free, like the wind that in the sky, aimlessly, writes.

Beyond the dawn, where dreams hide, lovers seek each other, call each other, respond to each other, in the silence of the night, their love is a cry, that pierces the shadows, a destiny written.

In each furtive encounter, in each farewell, they promise each other heaven, a shared life, although the world separates them with its cold law, they know that their love is stronger than their faith.

Like two comets in outer space, their passion drags them in a celestial dance, although they only meet when the stars align, their love is the force that sustains their souls.

And so, between struggle and resignation, they live their love with fervent devotion, knowing that even though they cannot be together, their love is a bond that breaks all walls.

In the twilight of their furtive encounters, where love is written in captive whispers, the souls of the lovers, in the distance, touch each other, and in each heartbeat, their hearts invoke.

They live in a world that does not understand their union, where their love is a verse in the song, a love that defies established rules, a love that in its essence, will never be defeated.

Through the centuries, their story is told, like a myth of passion that never absents, of two beings who, despite adversity, love each other with a force that defies reality.

In the darkness, they promise each other eternity, in each encounter, a sweet calamity, because even though destiny denies them the day, in their souls, their love would always be.

And so, the forbidden lovers continue their dance, in a dance of hope, full of trust, that someday, somewhere, their love will bloom, and in the light of the sun, at last, it will bathe.

XXVI

In the silence of a faded dream, where promises turn into oblivion,
there lies disappointment, cold and gloomy, like a winter that chills
the soul.

It is the echo of a love that breaks into pieces, they are the remains of
hopes in the arms, of those who gave everything without measure, and
found in return, the farewell.

Disappointment is a severe teacher, that teaches with pain, that is
sincere, it shows us that not everything is as it seems, that even the
most beautiful flower, sometimes withers.

It is the lost gaze on the horizon, it is the heart that no longer
responds, it is the emptiness that betrayal leaves, it is the silence after
the last song.

But even in disappointment there is a lesson, a path to strength and
reflection, it is learning to let go, to move forward, to transform pain
into vibrant art.

And so, the poem of disappointment is written, not as an end, but as
an incentive, to find in the ruins of what was, the seed of what will be,
and what is desired.

XXVII

Oh ebony muse, oh light of my day, in your gaze I found the sweetest
poetry, your laughter, the melody that ascends to heaven, and in each
of your gestures, time is suspended.
Your walk, graceful dance of the gentle breeze, that with each step,
magnifies my heart, you are the rose in eternal bloom, the only one,
whose aroma I always wish to have.
In the vastness of the night, your star shines brighter, illuminating my
shadows, guiding me in peace, and although destiny sometimes
separates us, in each verse, to you, my love I declare.
Your love, the beacon in my dark storm, the promise of a pure and safe
dawn,
in your arms, the refuge I always long for, my safe harbor, my sweet
comfort.
Oh my lady, in this sonnet I immortalize you, in each word, I
eternalize my love, and although my pen cannot capture your essence,
in my heart, I will always love you.
Your essence, oh beloved, is the canvas of my art, in each brushstroke,
my passion for you is shared, you are the light that guides my pen in
the darkness, the divine inspiration of my most sincere truth.
Each curl of your hair, a verse that slides, each of your smiles, a rhyme
that eternalizes, in the gallery of my heart, your portrait shines, and in
the museum of my soul, only your love prevails.
You are the tide that always returns to my shore, the force that
envelops my entire being, in the storm of life, my anchor and salvation,
the perfect melody in my song.

Oh lady of my dreams, my constant wakefulness, for you I would cross
the seas, I would reach the sky, and if words were lacking to express my
love, I would love you in silence, I would love you ceaselessly.
In each dawn, I see your face in the sun, and in each sunset, I feel your
calm in the afterglow, you are the promise of each new day, the eternal
source of my poetry.
Thus, my love for you, in these lines is poured, like a river that flows,
like the flame that calls, and even though I am no longer, my love for
you, in these verses, will always stand.
In each sigh of the night, I invoke your name, like a sacred mantra, a
crazy desire, you are the muse that appears in my dreams, the only
truth in this world that perishes.
Your beauty, oh beloved, defies nature, each curve of yours, a
masterpiece of purity, on the canvas of my life, your image is woven,
you are living poetry, the reason for my life.
In the theater of my mind, you are the main star, the heroine of a story
without end, and even though the curtains fall, the act ends, my love
for you, will eternally refine.
You are the whisper of the wind among the trees, the peace that is
found in the seas, and in this sonnet, I proclaim my love for you, like
Shakespeare, for his lady, an eternal claim.

XXVIII

In the mirror of the soul, the face appears, a portrait of emotions that
time takes, each line, each wrinkle, tells a story, of joys and sorrows
that life presents.
The eyes, windows of a wandering spirit, reflect the light of a flickering
love, gazes that speak without saying a word, in their depth, a passion
burns and carves.
Tears, pearls of pure melancholy, furrow the cheeks, in their sure fall,
they are the river that flows from the wounded heart, testimony of a
feeling, hidden in silence.

The lips, threshold of sighs and kisses, keep the secrets of captive loves, in their curve, the smile that has been lost, in their tremor, the desire that has been repressed.

The skin, canvas of life and its battles, each scar, a memory that does not shut up, it is the map of a journey, of struggle and passion, of moments lived with intense emotion.

And so, the face, reflection of existence, shows beauty in its purest essence, a visual poem, deep and sincere, that speaks in silence, that I hope in love.

In the silence of the skin, stories are shelled, each pore, a universe where souls emanate, the face, mirror of a deep inner world, where each emotion is revealed in a second.

The forehead, vast field of thoughts and dreams, where battles are fought, endeavors are forged, it is the stage of doubt and certainty, the cradle of the idea, the source of beauty.

The eyebrows, arches that frame the gaze, guardians of the window, through which the soul escapes, they are the prelude to the most sincere expression, the threshold of emotion, true passion.

And in the contour of the face, time leaves its mark, each furrow, a path that life seals, it is the dance of the years, the rhythm of existence, the song of being, the melody of consciousness.

Thus, the face becomes a living poem, a tale of love, of pain, of a latent feeling, a work of art forged by experience, a portrait of life, in its purest essence.

In the silence of the skin, stories are shelled, each pore, a universe where souls emanate, the face, mirror of a deep inner world, where each emotion is revealed in a second.

XXIX

Oh sea, vast being, eternal and deep, your waves sing to the secrets of
the world, in your blue embrace gazes are lost, and in your infinity,
souls fall in love.
You are the mirror where the sky is reflected, the cradle of life, the
voice that advises the earth, your waters, a temple of nameless
mysteries, a moonlit path, a dream that astonishes man.
In your depths, a universe hides, where time stands still, and space
responds, you are the pulse of the earth, its breath, the force that
moves creation with passion.
Oh sea, in your song, the history of the earth, of every creature, of
every war, your waves, the tears of those who have gone, the comfort
of those who have been defeated.

You are the altar where the sun offers its fire, and the moon, its silver, in an eternal game, sea, you are the poetry that never ends, the voice of Neruda that walks in the wind.

Oh sea, in your waters life is written, with each wave, a new promise is woven, you are the whisper of the earth at dawn, the refuge where the gods are reborn.

Your tides are the compass of the latent world, the embrace that envelops the brave traveler, in your deep blue, the secret is kept, of a love as great, as the entire universe.

You are the voice that sings in the vast solitude, the poet who narrates the eternal truth, sea, in your foam, sorrows are washed away, and in your salt, others' wounds are healed.

In the immensity of your being, I find peace, a spiritual connection that always satisfies, oh sea, you are the poem that will never cease, will always live.

XXX

The wind whispers ancient secrets, stories of times that were and will be, it is the messenger of the fatuous gods, the breath of the world that will never cease.
With each gust, a life awakens, in its caress, the promise of a new day, it is the artist who arranges in the sky, painting clouds in the vast gallery.
The wind, traveler of invisible routes, crosses mountains, valleys, rivers and seas, it is the embrace that unites impossible destinies, the bridge between dreams and places.
It carries in its dance the fallen leaves, plays with them in an endless waltz, it is the sigh of farewells, and the prelude of a boundless love.
It is the wind who dries the sad tears, who brings the aroma of the wet earth, who whispers to the lovers that you exist, who carries in its flight the soul in love.
Oh eternal wind, unstoppable force, that shapes the destiny with your vital breath, you are the voice that sings the ineffable, the melody that moves in its celestial singing.
The wind, in its eternal journey, tells stories of a lost past, whispers in the leaves, sings on the roof, it is the guardian of the secrets of the past.
With each breeze, it brings forgotten memories, of distant loves, of past times, it is the comfort of the lonely soul, the companion in the contrary night.
The wind carries life in its breath, from the gentle breeze to the ignited storm, it is the breath of nature, its creative force, the one who brings the rain, the one who devours the cloud.

It is the wind who speaks to us of freedom, who teaches us to fly in the
immensity, to let go of the moorings, to leave behind the fear, to feel
on the face the kiss of the sky.
Oh wind, you who transform everything, that with your breath shapes
the seasons, keep singing, keep blowing, keep moving the world, with
your endless dance.

XXXI

In the fabric of existence, humanity rises, with threads of compassion,
it shoes itself in its essence, a mosaic of souls, interwoven in diversity,
each life, a story, recorded in the book of time.
We should be the reflection of heaven on earth, bearers of peace, in the
midst of war, be the light that dispels the deepest darkness, the helping
hand, the voice that never sinks.
Humanity, a river of hope and love, where every gesture is a healing
act, where empathy is the currency of exchange, and respect, the
language we all speak.
We should be gardeners of the world we inhabit, sowing seeds of
kindness wherever we go, cultivating tolerance, harvesting unity, in the
farm of life, fraternity.

May spirituality be the wind that guides us, not as dogma, but as the
light that flows in the soul, that elevates us above ego and fear, and
unites us in the search for a new destiny.
Humanity, a choir of diverse voices, singing the song of the scattered
stars, that moves the reader, the dreamer, the traveler, that awakens in
every heart, the true warrior.
This is how the humanity we dream of should be, a canvas of love, on
which we all paint, a work of art that inspires each being, and on the
path of life, guides us all.

XXXII

In the game of chance, the lottery unfolds, with dancing numbers,
hope is given, each ticket, a dream printed on paper, on the wheel of
fortune, an express destiny.

Luck, capricious, laughs and flirts, in the draw of life, sometimes it
grants, sometimes it denies, it is the lottery, a dance of possibilities,
where illusion and reality cross their realities.

Some see in it the promise of a change, others, the reflection of a lost
desire, but everyone, at the time of the draw, holds their breath,
hoping that chance will give them a sweet moment.

The lottery, mirage of wealth and joy, in its essence, a metaphor for
daily life, it teaches us that not everything is winning or losing, but
knowing how to play, knowing how to live, knowing how to be.

And so, with each number, hope is renewed, in the great theater of the
world, the lottery rises, a poem to luck, to destiny, to perhaps, in the
draw of life, who will win?

The lottery, game of chance and destiny, where each number is a path,
a universe of possible stories, of ephemeral glories, of memories.

It is the echo of the hope that persists, in the heart of the dreamer who
insists, in the search for a stroke of luck, that changes their course, that
opens their door.

Each draw, a possibility in the wind, a sigh of thousands in a single
moment, the lottery, a reflection of life itself, where fortune is an
enigma, a mystery.

XXXIII

Faith, a beacon in the soul's night, the light that guides when life calms
down, it is the whisper of hope in the storm, the strength that in the
heart is cemented.

It is to believe in the invisible, in the intangible, in the promise of the
possible, the unimaginable.

Faith is the bridge between dream and reality, the breath that sustains
eternity.
In faith, we find the courage to be, to face fear, to be reborn, it is the
certainty in the depth of each being, that beyond the horizon, there is
a dawn.
Faith is the song of the bird before dawn, the conviction that is saved
in the spirit, it is the seed of a flourishing future, the conviction of an
omnipresent love.
And so, humanity clings to faith, like the anchor that is dropped in the
sea, it is the candle that lights up in the darkness,
the voice that understands the universe.
Faith, that compass in the uncertain journey, the anchor that keeps us
near the port, it is the flame that burns without seeing the wood, the
embrace we feel even though no one is waiting for us.
It is the firm step in the darkness, the hand we seek in solitude, faith is
the whisper that we are not alone, in the vast universe, in its infinite
corollas.
In faith, miracles find their cradle, in the act of believing, the fog
clears, it is the force that moves mountains, that calms seas, that leads
us to love, to overcome sorrows.
Faith is the poem that we never finish writing, the song that in the
soul does not cease to beat, it is the hope that tells us that it is worth it,
in every dawn, in every problem.
And so, humanity clings to faith, like the last grain of sand in the tide
that was gone,
it is the candle that lights up in the darkness, the voice that to the
universe understands and extends.
Faith, a whisper in the vastness of the cosmos, a golden thread in the
tapestry of immense time, it is the certainty in the darkest night, the
star that guides, the eternal adventure.

It is the embrace in the distance, the bridge over the abyss, the word of encouragement at the precise moment, faith is the fire that persists in the cold, the light that insists in the penumbra.

In faith, hearts meet, beyond the beliefs that segment us, it is the universal language, love without borders, unity in diversity, true peace.

Faith is the song of the soul that rises, the force that dares the impossible, it is the poetry that lives in every human being, the melody that unites us all and coexists.

And so, humanity clings to faith, like the castaway to the board that the sea gives him in his luck,

Until this moment, dear reader, we have sailed together through calm and clear waters, where poems, like gentle waves, have caressed us with their simplicity and tenderness.

We have enjoyed the light breeze that has brought us easy verses and sweet melodies, a prelude to what is to come.

Now, we delve into a deeper and vaster ocean, where the currents of poetry will lead us to explore abysses of thought and mountains of emotion. From this page onwards, the poems unfold like long and extensive fabrics, woven with threads of complex reflections and intense feelings.

Prepare to immerse yourself in the depth of verses that are like mighty rivers, whose waters flow with the strength of eternal truths and human passions.

Each poem will be a journey, an exploration of what it means to be alive, of what it means to love, to suffer, to hope, and to dream.

Open your heart and your mind, for what is coming is a feast of words, a labyrinth of metaphors where each turn is a revelation, and each stanza, a sigh of the soul.

These long and extensive poems are invitations to feel more deeply, to think more broadly, and to live more fully.

With high spirits and the pen ready, we begin this journey through the seas of deep poetry. May each word be one more step on our joint path towards the beauty and truth that lies in the art of verses.

I

I almost made it, I was on the verge, on the edge of destiny, on the
horizon, where feats rise like mountains, and the spirit is tested, strong
and forceful.

I was on the verge, at the pinnacle of the dream, where heroes and
legends are forged, in the forge of will, without a master, where each
step is an act that advocates.

I almost made it, in the dance of fire, where passion and desire
intertwine, in the embrace of life, without respite, where brave souls
embrace.

I was on the verge, in the relentless fight, where faith moves
mountains, awakens seas, where love is the prize, the laurel, and hope,
the light between suns and moons. I almost made it, in the whisper of
the wind, where the voices of the past whisper to me, where the future
is a canvas, an attempt, and the present, the battle that murmurs.

I was on the verge, and although I did not reach the summit, each
attempt was a victory, a lesson, in the book of life, each rhyme, is one
more step towards hope.

I almost made it, and I do not give up, for each fall is a new beginning,
and on the way, what I find and what I offer, is the reflection of a soul
that is priceless.

And I keep going, with a burning heart, in the relentless search for
that something more, where each defeat is a latent learning, and each
triumph, a step in the immensity.

I almost made it, in the echo of the battles, where glory and honor are not "vain", where each feat is a song that resonates in the souls, and each story, a legacy for the years.

I was on the verge, on the threshold of the eternal, where time stands still, and life expands, where the being meets the universe, and the truth is revealed, clear and great.

I almost made it, in the abyss of the unknown, where fear confronts, and courage distills, where destiny is written, and the path is chosen, and the will is affirmed, firm and calm.

I was on the verge, and I will be again, because the spirit longs, and the flame does not go out, on this endless journey, on this earthly dream, where each step is a verse, and life, a saga.

I almost made it, and although the end is uncertain, passion guides me, and love sustains me, in this dance of stars, in this open universe, where each soul is a poem, that the cosmos contains.

And so, in the depth of existence, where the soul plunges into mystery, each beat is an echo of consciousness, and each sigh, a reflection of the infinite.

I almost made it, in the stillness of the night, where the stars tell ancestral stories, where silence speaks, and the heart listens, and each thought is a bridge between parallel worlds.

I was on the verge, in the immensity of the ocean, where each wave is a melody of creation, where the horizon merges with the sky, and passion becomes a prayer.

I almost made it, in the intimacy of being, where the truth is stripped bare, and the essence is revealed, where love is the only language, and the only duty, and life, a sacred and beautiful dance.

I was on the verge, and I continue in the search, because each step is a discovery, and each moment, an opportunity to be light, on this path of self-discovery.

I almost made it, and my spirit rises, in the aspiration to reach the sublime, where each test is a call to the soul, and each victory, a song that redeems.

And in the journey of the soul, with no marked end, where each step is a verse in the poem of the universe, the light of the stars guides my encrypted path, and each dream is an immersed desire.

I almost made it, in the serenity of dawn, where the rising sun promises a new day, where hope is reborn, and nothing ends, and each beat of the heart is a melody.

I was on the verge, in the whisper of the breeze, where nature sings its eternal song, where beauty unfolds, and life improvises, and each moment is a page that turns.

I almost made it, in the strength of the spirit, where determination forges character, where courage becomes a cry, and each challenge is a chapter that makes me stronger.

I was on the verge, and my journey continues, because destiny is a canvas to paint, and in the art of living, the work is one, where each brushstroke is an act of love.

I almost made it, and the search never ceases, because in the mystery of life, everything is possible, and in the heart of existence, beauty, is an endless poem, sublime and unspeakable.

And the saga continues, with each breath, in the plot of life, the thread tightens, where each act is a moment, and each word, a promise.

I almost made it, in the light of each star, where the universe whispers ancient secrets, where wisdom is a spark that shines, and each truth, a treasure we keep.

I was on the verge, in the harmony of the cosmos, where everything is a dance of pure energy, where the being merges with the whole, without dregs, and each existence, a safe adventure.

I almost made it, in the reflection of the mirror, where I see myself,
and everything I have been, where the past and the future intertwine
in a fabric, and each experience, a learning that I collect.
I was on the verge, and there is no end to this story, because each end
is a beginning, and each closure an opening, in this endless cycle, in
this search for glory, where each step is a stroke in the painting.
I almost made it, and my soul does not despair, because in the poetry
of life, each verse is a breath, and on the canvas of time, each color is a
wait, where each brushstroke is a feeling.
And the saga continues, with each breath, in the plot of life, the thread
tightens, where each act is a moment, and each word, a promise.

II

In the serenity of dawn, where the rising sun promises a new day, the
light seeps in, soft and calm, and in its embrace, the cold night
deviates.
The sky is dyed with vivid colors, pinks, oranges, on an unparalleled
canvas, the world awakens, in captive whispers, and hope is renewed,
naturally.
The birds sing their melodies, greeting the sun king in his ascent, the
morning breeze brings comfort and joys, and the soul is filled with
immense silence.
It is the moment of new beginnings, of dreams that have been forged
in the night, it is the time of intense desires, of plans and renewed
projects.
In the serenity of dawn, everything is possible, the horizon opens, wide
and generous, each moment is valuable and priceless, and the heart
feels free and joyful.
Thus, in the tranquility of the morning, where each drop of dew is a
treasure, life presents itself, clear and healthy, and in the new day, each
being feels decorous.

In the quiet of dawn, the world is renewed, each ray of light, a caress that awakens, the sky, a poem that the sun writes and elevates, and the earth, a canvas where life is inserted.
The breeze carries aromas of distant lands, whispers of waves, of mountains and valleys, each breath, a story that sister souls, share in silence, among whispers and details.
The horizon is dressed with the promise of the day, a mantle of hope woven with threads of light, each moment, a jewel that life sends, and each dream, a path that seduces the heart.
In the serenity of dawn, passion is unleashed, like a river that flows, powerful and endless, nature sings, and each note portrays, the infinite beauty that is kept here, in the garden.
Thus, at each dawn, the charm is renewed, life presents itself with its mysteries and its art, in each new day, there is a reason for the song, and in each beat of the soul, that leaves.
And in the dance of dawn, life unfolds, with each ray of sun, a canvas is illuminated, the world awakens, and nature delivers, its symphony of colors, on a divine palette.
The serenity of dawn, a temple of quietude, where the soul finds peace and the spirit is inspired, each shine of the sky, a message of fullness, and each bird's song, a melody that does not expire.

In the promise of the day, strength is renewed, hope dresses in light, and courage is affirmed, each dream is nourished by the faith that rises, and each step forward, a story that is confirmed.

Thus, in the serenity of dawn, each being reveals itself, in the masterpiece of creation, each one is an artist, painting his destiny with brushstrokes that console, in the art of living, every day is a conquest. And so, with the light of dawn as a guide, the path of life becomes clear, each step a promise, each day, a gift that destiny puts at our disposal.

The serenity of dawn, a song of hope, a whisper of the earth that invites us to be reborn, each ray of sun, a spear that breaks the darkness, teaching us to see.
In the calm of dawn, each heart opens, receiving the new day with extended arms, the beauty of the world, subtle and soft, is revealed in the most hidden details.
Thus, in the silence of the early morning, where time seems to stop and wait, each being finds itself, each soul becomes a sister, in the eternal dance of living and dreaming.
And the poem flows, like the river to the sea, in the serenity of dawn, life awakens, each new sun, a challenge to face, an opportunity for the soul to discover itself open.
The calm of dawn, a blank canvas, where each color is a dream to paint, hope rises, without rank, and on the horizon, a destiny to reach.
In the soft light of the day that is born, the promises of a thousand tomorrows are hidden, each ray of sun, a trace, that illuminates the paths, removes the desires.
Thus, in the tranquility of this new beginning, where nature whispers its song, each moment is an immense treasure, and each step, a new direction.
The serenity of dawn, a song to the heart, where each beat is a verse of the universe, and we, the dreamers, with devotion, continue writing the most diverse poem.

Beyond the dawn, where dreams hide, in the realm of silence, where legends are born, each feat is a whisper that the shadows welcome, and each deed, a story that the times link.
In the twilight of dawn, the heroes awaken, with the strength of the seas and the calm of the breeze, their steps resonate, on the uncertain earth, and their courage rises, like a precise promise.

The feats are woven, on the tapestry of destiny, where each thread is an act of courage and faith, where glory is not an end, but a path, and each victory, a legacy that does not unravel.
Beyond the dawn, at the peak of the day, where the sun illuminates the highest peaks, dreams are forged, with passion and harmony, and each achievement, a story that never lacks.

In the heart of the battle, hope ignites, like a flame that never extinguishes or surrenders, each struggle, an epic that the soul understands, and each triumph, an echo that expands in eternity.
Beyond the dawn, where dreams hide, each being is a poet, each life a poetry, and on the canvas of time, the feats respond, with the ink of life, writing the odyssey of the day.
In the twilight of being, where fears lurk, a man faces the reflection of his soul, each fear, a shadow that despises him, and each doubt, a storm that calms him down.
Beyond the dawn, in the labyrinth of his mind, where dreams and fears are confused, he seeks the light, a truth that guides him, and a courage that floods his own ghosts.
With each step, uncertainty challenges him, in the mirror, his eyes reflect the struggle, against himself, the most secret battle, where overcoming oneself is the feat he listens to.
The man fears the monster within, that dark passenger of his thoughts, but in his heart, a fire has been lit, and he is determined to break his own foundations.

Beyond the dawn, where hope waits, he rises, with the strength of a thousand suns, facing his fears, which no longer intimidate him, overcoming them, he achieves his desires and roles.

And in the victory over himself, he finds peace, the serenity of dawn, his new ally, each fear overcome, a step that makes him capable, of living life, without being bound by fear.
And in the silence that follows the storm, the man rises, stronger and more determined, each fear faced, a door that opens, and each shadow defeated, a path traveled.
Beyond the dawn, where the light hides, he finds his refuge, his inner sanctuary, where each battle won responds to him, and each step forward, an eternal destiny. In the struggle against himself, he discovers his power, the ability to change, to grow and to be, each fear overcome, a step to ascend, and each doubt dispelled, an opportunity to see.
The man faces the mirror of his soul, and sees not an enemy, but a friend, a guide, each fear, a lesson that calms, and each victory, a melody.
Beyond the dawn, in the clarity of the day, he walks with confidence, with his head held high, each fear left behind, a wisdom, and each step forward, a life lived.

III

Flare of a Goodbye
In the twilight of our love, the flames danced, burning like the desire that once consumed us. It was you, the living flame nested in my chest, which in a whisper of passion, transformed my being.
Your absence, an eclipse in my clear sky, left my world in shadows, my sun without its glow.

Each beat, an echo of the love we have silenced, each memory, a
shooting star that lost its color.
I look for you in every verse that the wind takes, in every word that the
night steals from me. You are the lost dream, the promise that breaks,
the passion that in my soul, eternally, unfolds.
I sail in a sea of tears, in the storm of your goodbye, where each wave is
a kiss, each drop, a lost moment.
In the high tide of my pain, I cry out for your voice, for that love that
left, leaving me wounded. Your memory still burns, a fire that does not
go out, in the fireplace of my memory, where you still dance.
And even though cruel fate unravels our union, you will always be the
passion that subjugated my life.
In the penumbra of my room, I feel you, like a whisper from the past
that does not want to leave.
Your laughter, a distant echo carried by the wind, and your gaze, a
memory that makes me suffer.
Tears of fire, soak my pillow, each one, a memory of the golden days.
Days when your love embraced my life, now only torn dreams remain.
I miss you in every dawn, in every sunset, in every star that in the sky I
can count. Although I try to move forward, step by step, your absence
is an abyss that I cannot jump.
I promised you eternal love, and I still hold it, even though cruel fate
tore you from my side. My heart keeps the oath I have to you, to love
you beyond death, I have sworn it.
Although today my world is broken and gloomy, a spark of hope
shines in the darkness. Perhaps in another life, in another river, our
love will be reborn, pure and simple.
My voice rises in the night, a song to the void, seeking the echo of your
laughter, the warmth of your skin.
In every shadow, I pursue you, a somber desire, in every silence, I
invoke you, my lost Eden.

Your image, a portrait that time does not fade, remains immortal in the gallery of my mind.

Each stroke, a caress that exalts the heart, each color, a feeling that eternally feels.

Loneliness, my only faithful companion, mute witness to my love that does not surrender.

In its cold embrace, I find the cruel memory of a love that fate extinguishes.

Under the tearful moon, I look for you among the stars, in each one, a desire, in each light, a hope.

Although the night is dark and the shadows are the ones that speak to me of you, in my heart there is no balance.

This elegy I write to the lost passion, to the kisses that left, to the dreams that died.

In each word, a hidden tear,

In every line, the sighs that left us.

In the mist of my mind, your words resonate, like distant bells that time cannot silence.

They are, the voices that in my solitude alienate me, the ones that speak to me of you, the ones I cannot forget. Like a footprint in the sand that the tide erases, so fades the trace of your love. But on the beach of my soul, your memory emerges, indelible, perpetual, marking the pain.

The scent of your perfume still invades my space, a sweet ghost of happier days. It is a balm and at the same time a wretched omen, that reminds me of what was and what is no longer.

I sing to you in silence, a lullaby for the dream, that we shared, that now only I must lull. It is the melody of a love that was master, of my heart, of my life, of my eternity.

On the bridge where we said goodbye, where our souls for the last time met, there I leave my tears, my sighs, and the promise to love you, until the worlds end.

In the silence of the night, your echoes resonate, songs of love that still persist in my soul. They are melodies of a past that my tears bathe, memories of you that insist in my heart.
I still feel the trace of your essence in my being, a perfume that refuses to fade.
It is the indelible trace of a love, that although absent, teaches me to be reborn.
Under the light of the moon, I contemplate you in dreams, your image clear like the crystalline river. In the lunar quietude, I feel you close, without owners, in an ethereal dance, our love is a challenge.
I promised you eternal love, and in eternity I fulfill it,
even though you are far away, my heart does not know forgetfulness.
In every star, in every sigh, in every lullaby, my love for you, firm and perpetual, has promised.
And if this were the last goodbye, let it be in poetry, a goodbye that does not end, that lives in verses. Because even though life separates us, my soul still, in every word, in every rhyme,
revives for you.

IV

Face to face, under the starry mantle, our gazes meet, they recognize each other. The fire dances, witness to a consecrated love, while spiritual songs intertwine in the air.
Around the fire, the voices rise, ancestral songs that awaken the spirit.
But in the center, only you and I, without reservations, in a universe of our own, where souls are right

.

Your eyes, two universes in which I lose myself,
reflect the passion that my whole being claims. In them I see love, pure and tender, and in this sacred moment, my heart proclaims you.

While the flames confide their secrets to the sky, and the voices around the fire profess their faith, we, in silence, love each other in poetry, in an eternal language that the soul expresses.

In this circle of light, of heat and song, where the earthly and the divine merge endlessly, our love is celebrated, strong and holy, in an embrace of gazes that seals our destiny.
Under the sky of witnesses, the stars twinkle, observing our love, as vast as the night. Around the fire, the souls fan, but in your arms, I find my extravagance.
The flames whisper an ancient melody, a song that accompanies the beating of two hearts. In this ritual of gazes, our own league, we seal a pact beyond reasons.
Our eyes interlace in a silent dance, a language that only our souls understand. While the spiritual choir raises its song, our love, in the glow of the fire, ignites.
The fire crackles, like my desire for you, each spark, a reflection of our burning passion. In this sacred circle, I feel free, I feel yes, because with you, every moment is a present.
And on this night, where time seems to stop, where each song is a thread that unites us, your gaze and mine, in an embrace that wants to be seen, promise a love that not even the universe overthrows.
In the mirror of your eyes, I see eternity, a love that transcends the here and now. Around us, the spiritual song in its purity, and we, in the center, where time fades.
We are the heart of the circle, the core of the fire, where the flames of love and life intertwine.
The voices around are a river that flows without ego, but on our island, love is the only trace.
The moon bathes us with its silver light, blessing this encounter of twin souls.

While the sacred choir accompanies our union, our hearts swear love without truce.

The fire crackles, the voices rise, a song of love that the universe intones.

And in this sacred moment, our souls dance, in a promise of love that fertilizes everything.

Your gaze ignites in me an immortal fire, a passion that not even the largest ocean could extinguish.

In this divine moment, our love is a ritual, a moment of connection that I will always treasure.

V

In the silence of the night, together but alone, curled up in the bed of paradox and desire. She, with her heart on fire, he, her comfort, in an embrace that is a refuge, but also a challenge.
So close that their breaths mingle, as far away as the stars in the sky. Each touch is a whisper of what could not be, of a deep love, trapped in flight.
Every time they get closer, the world stops, a magnetism that reason cannot explain. She, lost in the gaze of the one who loves her well, he, the force that attracts her, her eternal sea.
They are lovers in the shadows, without being so, united by a feeling they cannot name.
She, in love with every gesture, every hair, he, the presence that comes to calm her soul.
It's a sweet pain, to love in silence, to want without being able to have, without being able to shout.
She, with every beat, feels the dense weight of a love that life does not let prosper.
And so, in the bed where they share dreams, where passion disguises itself as mere company, she wonders if desires are masters of changing destiny, of giving light to the day.
In the bed where they lie, two souls in silence, share dreams and sighs, but no promises.
She, with a heart overflowing with feeling, he, the presence that confesses her love.

Every movement is a delicate dance, a game of proximity that destiny denies them.

She, with every touch, feels more in love, he, the calm in the storm, where his heart surrenders.

It's a love that lives in the limbo of the unspoken, in the space between the sheets and the skin.

She, with every breath, feels the spell, of a love that, although forbidden, is faithful.

Curled up in the paradox of their reality, where love is a fire they cannot extinguish.

She, with a gaze full of truth, he, the dream he does not want to wake up from.

In the embrace that says everything without words, where warmth is a language that both understand.

She, in the tenderness of his arms, finds the answer to a love that fears do not ignite.

In the bed where love hides, two bodies speak in the silence of the night.

She, with a love that responds in her chest, he, the presence that ignites and squanders her passion.

Curled up in time, in a love without time, where each caress is a verse that has not been written.

She, with a heart that overflows and breathless, he, the calm in her storm, his perfect rite.

In the labyrinth of sheets, they find themselves lost, a desire that is sought, but never found. She, with a love that is a forbidden fire, he, the reason that escapes, the one that is absent.

On the skin, stories are told of a forbidden love, stories of a love that only lives in dreams.

She, with every touch, feels that she is lost, he, the map of a treasure that destiny evades.

In the embrace that holds the world and its mysteries, where love is a language that only they speak. She, in his arms, finds her sanctuaries, he, in his love, the fears that disavow.
In the quiet of the night, our bodies approach, a silent echo of a love that blooms in the shadow. She, with a heart that tightens by his side, he, the presence that seems her eternal love.
Curled up in destiny, in a love without destiny, where each sigh is a poem that has not been read. She, with a love that is a river without a path,
he, the shore that sustains her, his hidden secret
In the labyrinth of their hearts, they find themselves confused, a desire that is sought, but always evades. She, with a love that is an unlit fire, he, the spark that is missing, the one that the wind persuades.
On the skin, stories are told of a contained love, stories of a love that is only allowed in intimacy.
She, with every touch, feels that she is blessed, he, the temple of her adoration, her infinite love.
In the embrace that holds the soul and its secrets, where love is a language that only they know.
She, in his arms, finds her complete refuges, he, in his love, the fears that strip away.

VI

In the silence of the night, my pen awakens, to weave words of a love on alert. A man, wandering on his path, seeks his destiny in verses.
In the twilight of a love that fades, a man cries out to the sky that does not dawn. With his soul in ruins, his heart in tears, he searches in the stars, for the forgiveness he so desires.
"Forgive me," he whispers to the wind, "for the wounds I caused without intent. For every tear that was born in your eyes, for the trust that day by day died."

In the passion of a lost embrace, he remembers the warmth they
shared. The touch of her skin, the whisper of her voice,
the promise of a forever, between him and us.
"Come back to me," he begs the moon, "let me be your sun, your only
fortune. I want to be the guardian of your dreams, the architect of a
future without owners."
With each verse, he tries to put back together, the puzzle of his love.
Each word, a brick of hope, to build a castle, without balance.
"I love you," he declares with fervor,
"beyond the pain, beyond the error.
You are the tide that guides my boat,
the light that in my darkness, marks."
Thus, with a poem woven of passion, he seeks to redeem his
transgression. A man who failed, but who still breathes, for a love that
endures, that inspires.
May this poem be the echo of his soul, a song of love that calms the
night. A man who fails, but who still desires, to recover the woman he
loves, he longs for.
In the quiet of his being, the man contemplates, the vastness of a sky
that does not lament.
"Where are you, love, on this starry night? In what corner of the
world, is my fault repaired?"
"I look for you among the people, on every corner, with the hope that
destiny will align us. I would like to turn back time, change the story,
to not be the villain in our memory."
"I remember your smile, like a radiant sun,
In the silence of the night, my pen awakens, to weave words of a love
on alert. A man, wandering on his path, seeks his destiny in verses.
In the twilight of his mistake, the man waits, with the faith of a
believer, in the austere chapel.
"Will you listen, my love, to this painful song? Will you forgive the
past, embrace the present?"

"I offer you my being, without masks or veils, an open heart, free of worries. I want to be the refuge in your storm, the faithful companion, that faces your loneliness."

"For every wrong step, I have planted a flower, in the garden of our love, now renewed. For every broken dream, I have hung a star, in the firmament of promises, illuminated by you."

"Let my love be your shield, against the world, against everything crude. Let my passion be the fire that warms you, on cold nights, when loneliness obliges you."

"Come, let me be the poetry on your skin, the perfect verse, the sweet honey. Let me be the melody in your song, the rhythm that accompanies, your heart."

"Together, we can write a new story, one without sad endings, full of glory. Where you and I are the protagonists, in a love that surpasses, all lists."

"This poem is my voice, my sincere prayer, for a future together, without separation. A man who fails, but who gets up, for a love that forgives, that endures everything."

May these words be the whisper in your ear, the warm embrace, the reborn love. So that when you read them, you feel in your heart, the true love, without condition.

At the dawn of a new day, the man awakens, with the hope of a love that reinvents itself.

"Wake up, my love, with the light of dawn, where every mistake is erased and saved."

"I want to be the sun that dries your tears, the gentle wind that calms your fears.

To be the sigh of relief in your days, the certainty of love in your empty nights."

"For every word that hurt, I have saved a kiss, in the chest of my desires, safeguarded for you.

For every silence that weighed, a song I have composed, to fill with melody, the emptiness of our nest."

"Let my love be the breeze that caresses you, the embrace that in the distance, shelters you. Let my passion be the flame that never goes out, the eternal fire, that distinguishes itself in your heart."

"Come, let me be the ink in your story, the happy chapter, the memory. Let me be the peace in your torment, the safe refuge, the sweet moment."

"Together, we can defy every storm, build a love that life nourishes. Where you and I are the perfect reflection, in a love that is pure, without any defect."

"This poem is my extended hand, my open heart, my life. A man who fails, but who adores you, for a love that revives, that now implores."

May these words be the light on your path, the beacon that guides, the divine destiny.

So that by following it, you find in me, the unconditional love, that I always promised you.

VII

In the universe of two outstretched palms, secrets are found, uncomprehended stories. Hands that speak, that caress existence, with the delicacy of a loving science.

Hands that narrate, in each line, a life, in each scar, a battle won. They are the brush that paints emotions in the air, the instrument that composes, without disdain.

"Hands of my beloved," whispers the lover, "they are the refuge where my soul rises. Your fingers, the verses of my favorite poem, your palm, the canvas of our infinite love."

Hands that feel, that tremble and yearn, that seek in the skin, the passion that one day cooled. They are the fire that burns, without fear of consuming itself, the promise of a touch, that refuses to extinguish.

"Hands that explore," sings the poet, "they are the compass of a heart in vendetta. Your caresses, the map to the lost treasure, your touch, the path I have always followed."

Hands that unite, that intertwine destinies, that write in the other, their most divine verses. They are the bridge between two lonely souls, the strength that sustains, daily hopes.

"Intertwined hands," declares the lover, "they are the symbol of a vibrant love. Your presence, the certainty in my uncertainty, your support, the pillar in my collapse."

Hands that heal, that cure wounds, that offer themselves generously, never divided. They are the balm that soothes the deepest pain, the silence that accompanies, in the mourning of the world.

"Hands that console," prays the believer, "they are tangible faith, the gentle gesture. Your touch, the prayer that calms my torment, your embrace, the temple of my contentment."

Hands that speak, without the need for words, that say "I love you," on the clearest nights. They are the voice of the heart, when fear silences, the whisper of love, that in the distance is silent.

"Hands that seek each other," dreams the poet, "they are the melody that my soul completes. Your signal, the answer to my questions, your gesture, the peace that my battles point to."

Thus, in the dance of hands that meet, a love story is woven that is not told. Hands that are the refuge, the passion, the promise, the universal language, the beauty that begins.

In the symphony of life, hands continue their song, a hymn of eternal love, that defies crying. Hands that promise, in every gesture, an eternity, in every touch, the story of a city. Hands that give, without expecting to receive, that offer the world, without asking. They are the gift of a generous soul, silent charity, the precious rose.

"Hands of my life," cries the wounded heart, "they are the cure for my ills, the chosen path. Your fingers, the pillars of my strength, your palm, the sanctuary of my nature."

Hands that create, that shape the future,
In the universe of two outstretched hands, secrets are found, stories not understood. Hands that speak, that caress existence, with the delicacy of a loving science.
Hands that narrate, in each line, a life, in each scar, a battle won. They are the brush that paints emotions in the air, the instrument that composes, without disdain.
"Hands of my beloved," whispers the lover, "they are the refuge where my soul rises. Your fingers, the verses of my favorite poem, your palm, the canvas of our infinite love."
Hands that feel, that tremble and yearn, that seek in the skin, the passion that one day cooled. They are the fire that burns, without fear of consuming itself, the promise of a touch, that refuses to extinguish.
"Hands that explore," sings the poet, "they are the compass of a heart in vendetta. Your caresses, the map to the lost treasure, your touch, the path I have always followed."
Hands that unite, that intertwine destinies, that write in the other, their most divine verses. They are the bridge between two lonely souls, the strength that sustains, daily hopes.
"Intertwined hands," declares the lover, "they are the symbol of a vibrant love. Your presence, the certainty in my uncertainty, your support, the pillar in my collapse."
Hands that heal, that cure wounds, that offer themselves generously, never divided. They are the balm that soothes the deepest pain, the silence that accompanies, in the mourning of the world.
"Hands that console," prays the believer, "they are tangible faith, the gentle gesture. Your touch, the prayer that calms my torment, your embrace, the temple of my contentment."
Hands that speak, without the need for words, that say "I love you," on the clearest nights. They are the voice of the heart, when fear silences, the whisper of love, that in the distance is silent.

"Hands that seek each other," dreams the poet, "they are the melody that my soul completes. Your signal, the answer to my questions, your gesture, the peace that my battles point to."
Thus, in the dance of hands that meet, a love story is woven that is not told. Hands that are the refuge, the passion, the promise, the universal language, the beauty that begins.
In the symphony of life, hands continue their song, a hymn of eternal love, that defies crying.
Hands that promise, in every gesture, an eternity, in every touch, the story of a city. Hands that give, without expecting to receive, that offer the world, without asking.
They are the gift of a generous soul, silent charity, the precious rose.

"Hands of my life," cries the wounded heart, "they are the cure for my ills, the chosen path. Your fingers, the pillars of my strength, your palm, the sanctuary of my nature."
Hands that create, that shape the future, that write in the cosmos, a secure destiny. They are the chisel that sculpts dreams in stone, the will that in the void, sows.
"Hands that build," celebrates the craftsman, "they are the masterpiece of a sovereign plan. Your works, the legacy of our passion, your skill, the fruit of inspiration."
Hands that protect, that defend the loved one, that guard the treasure, forever guarded. They are the shield against adversity, the promise of security, in the storm.
"Hands that guard," trusts the warrior, "they are the fortress of my whole world. Your bravery, the light in my battle, your firmness, the victory that does not keep silent."
Hands that speak of love, in each caress, that tell a legend, in each delight. They are the expression of the purest feeling, the dialogue of two souls, on the sure path.

"Hands that express themselves," sighs the lover, "they are the poetry that recites the moment. Your contact, the word that does not need sound, your gesture, the message that I have always wanted."
In the universe of two hands that seek each other, a love is discovered that breaks through barriers. Hands that are the refuge, the passion, the truth, the universal language, eternity.
In the theater of life, hands continue their work, a tale of passion, that the soul unfolds. Hands that whisper, in each touch, a secret, in each squeeze, the warmth of an affection.
Hands that promise, in each promise, a future, in each support, a secure love. They are the oath of two intertwined hearts, the certainty of two aligned destinies.
"Hands that commit," longs the dreamer, "they are the pact of a love without fear. Your fingers, the seals of our union, your palm, the refuge of my passion."
Hands that discover, that seek and find, that reveal in the skin, stories that are told. They are the adventure that never ends, the exploration of a love that dominates.
"Hands that investigate," explores the lover, "they are the odyssey of a constant feeling. Your caresses, the discovery of my joy, your touch, the map of our harmony."
Hands that give themselves, that give without measure, that offer their being, without any departure. They are the gift of a total surrender, the promise of a special bond.
"Hands that give," offers the faithful, "they are the display of a love that is heaven. Your presence, the most precious gift, your support, the most valued treasure."

Hands that communicate, that speak without sounds,
that express "I love you," in the moments lived.
They are the conversation of the soul, when words are lacking, the
dialogue of love, that breaks through barriers.

"Hands that dialogue," converses the poet, "they are the chat that my heart interprets. Your signal, the communication of our desires, your gesture, the understanding of our longings."

In the concert of two hands that communicate, a love is discovered that shortens distances. Hands that are the refuge, the passion, the message, the universal language, the eternal journey.

In the silence of the night, hands continue their dialogue, a whisper of love, that crosses the monologue. Hands that tell, in each touch, a story, in each hug, a memory.

Hands that call, that invite to union, that gestate in the air, the sweetest song.

They are the call of two souls that seek each other, the signal of two hearts that listen to each other.

"Hands that invoke," asks the lover, "they are the song of a constant love. Your fingers, the threads of our connection, your palm, the altar of my devotion."

Hands that give life, that sow and care, that in the fertile earth, love and hope nest. They are the source of a love that blooms, the garden of an affection that never decreases.

"Hands that cultivate," works the gardener, "they are the essence of a sincere love. Your gestures, the seeds of our tomorrow,

In the universe of two outstretched hands, secrets are found, stories not understood. Hands that speak, that caress existence, with the delicacy of a loving science.

Hands that narrate, in each line, a life, in each scar, a battle won. They are the brush that paints emotions in the air, the instrument that composes, without disdain.

"Hands of my beloved," whispers the lover, "they are the refuge where my soul rises. Your fingers, the verses of my favorite poem, your palm, the canvas of our infinite love."

Hands that feel, that tremble and yearn, that seek in the skin, the passion that one day cooled. They are the fire that burns, without fear of consuming itself, the promise of a touch, that refuses to extinguish.
"Hands that explore," sings the poet, "they are the compass of a heart in vendetta. Your caresses, the map to the lost treasure, your touch, the path I have always followed."
Hands that unite, that intertwine destinies, that write in the other, their most divine verses. They are the bridge between two lonely souls, the strength that sustains, daily hopes.
"Intertwined hands," declares the lover, "they are the symbol of a vibrant love. Your presence, the certainty in my uncertainty, your support, the pillar in my collapse."
Hands that heal, that cure wounds, that offer themselves generously, never divided. They are the balm that soothes the deepest pain, the silence that accompanies, in the mourning of the world.
"Hands that console," prays the believer, "they are tangible faith, the gentle gesture. Your touch, the prayer that calms my torment, your embrace, the temple of my contentment."
Hands that speak, without the need for words, that say "I love you," on the clearest nights. They are the voice of the heart, when fear silences, the whisper of love, that in the distance is silent.
"Hands that seek each other," dreams the poet, "they are the melody that my soul completes. Your signal, the answer to my questions, your gesture, the peace that my battles point to."
Thus, in the dance of hands that meet, a love story is woven that is not told. Hands that are the refuge, the passion, the promise, the universal language, the beauty that begins.
In the symphony of life, hands continue their song, a hymn of eternal love, that defies crying. Hands that promise, in every gesture, an eternity, in every touch, the story of a city.

Hands that give, without expecting to receive, that offer the world, without asking. They are the gift of a generous soul, silent charity, the precious rose.

"Hands of my life," cries the wounded heart, "they are the cure for my ills, the chosen path. Your fingers, the pillars of my strength, your palm, the sanctuary of my nature."

Hands that create, that shape the future, that write in the cosmos, a secure destiny. They are the chisel that sculpts dreams in stone, the will that in the void, sows.

"Hands that build," celebrates the craftsman, "they are the masterpiece of a sovereign plan. Your works, the legacy of our passion, your skill, the fruit of inspiration."

Hands that protect, that defend the loved one, that guard the treasure, forever guarded. They are the shield against adversity, the promise of security, in the storm.

"Hands that guard," trusts the warrior, "they are the fortress of my whole world. Your bravery, the light in my battle, your firmness, the victory that does not keep silent."

Hands that speak of love, in each caress, that tell a legend, in each delight. They are the expression of the purest feeling, the dialogue of two souls, on the sure path.

"Hands that express themselves," sighs the lover, "they are the poetry that recites the moment. Your contact, the word that does not need sound, your gesture, the message that I have always wanted."

In the universe of two hands that seek each other, a love is discovered that breaks through barriers. Hands that are the refuge, the passion, the truth, the universal language, eternity.

In the theater of life, hands continue their work, a tale of passion, that the soul unfolds. Hands that whisper, in each touch, a secret, in each squeeze, the warmth of an affection.

Hands that promise, in each promise, a future, in each support, a secure love. They are the oath of two intertwined hearts, the certainty of two aligned destinies.

"Hands that commit," longs the dreamer, "they are the pact of a love without fear. Your fingers, the seals of our union, your palm, the refuge of my passion."

Hands that discover, that seek and find, that reveal in the skin, stories that are told. They are the adventure that never ends, the exploration of a love that dominates. "Hands that investigate,"

explores the lover, "they are the odyssey of a constant feeling. Your caresses, the discovery of my joy, your touch, the map of our harmony." Hands that give themselves, that give without measure, that offer their being, without any departure. They are the gift of a total surrender, the promise of a special bond.

"Hands that give," offers the faithful, "they are the display of a love that is heaven. Your presence, the most precious gift, your support, the most valued treasure."

Hands that communicate, that speak without sounds, that express "I love you," in the moments lived. They are the conversation of the soul, when words are lacking, the dialogue of love, that breaks through barriers.

"Hands that dialogue," converses the poet, "they are the chat that my heart interprets. Your signal, the communication of our desires, your gesture, the understanding of our longings."

In the concert of two hands that communicate, a love is discovered that shortens distances. Hands that are the refuge, the passion, the message, the universal language, the eternal journey.

In the silence of the night, hands continue their dialogue, a whisper of love, that crosses the monologue. Hands that tell, in each touch, a story, in each hug, a memory.

Hands that call, that invite to union, that gestate in the air, the sweetest song.

They are the call of two souls that seek each other, the signal of two hearts that listen to each other.

"Hands that invoke," asks the lover, "they are the song of a constant love. Your fingers, the threads of our connection, your palm, the altar of my devotion."

Hands that give life, that sow and care, that in the fertile earth, love and hope nest. They are the source of a love that blooms, the garden of an affection that never decreases.

"Hands that cultivate," works the gardener, "they are the essence of a sincere love. Your gestures, the seeds of our tomorrow, your care, the harvest that the soul wins."

Hands that say goodbye, that let go with regret, that in the goodbye, promise to find again. They are the bridge between the now and the reunion, the hope of a future, the central feeling.

"Hands that move away," cries the traveler, "they are the promise of a true love. Your goodbye, the prelude to a new beginning, your return, the chapter of an immense love."

Hands that celebrate, that applaud and dance, that in every victory, throw a joy. They are the expression of a shared joy, the celebration of an achievement, achieved by both.

"Hands that celebrate," laughs the companion, "they are the melody of a sincere love. Your jubilation, the song of our union, your dance, the rhythm of my heart."

In the theater of two hands that meet, a love story is narrated that words do not tell. Hands that are the refuge, the passion, the celebration, the universal language, the purest emotion.

At the dawn of a new dream, hands take flight, a journey of love, that takes off from the ground. Hands that dream, in each elevation, a hope, in each union, a dance.

Hands that ascend, that reach heights, that draw in the clouds, their adventures. They are the wing of a desire that rises, the freedom of a love that dares.

"Hands that fly," aspires the dreamer, "they are the takeoff of a love without fear. Your fingers, the wings of our passion, your palm, the sky of my devotion."
Hands that imagine, that create new worlds, that in fantasy, know no brakes. They are the magic of a story that comes to life, the illusion of a love that never forgets.
"Hands that draw," fantasizes the artist, "they are the work of a love without a list. Your strokes, the canvas of our story, your creativity, the source of our glory."
Hands that rise, that overcome barriers, that in adversity, are the first. They are the impulse of a love that does not give up, the flight of a heart that lights up.
"Hands that rise," encourages the brave, "they are the strength of a present love. Your elevation, the triumph over fear, your height, the refuge where I stay."
Hands that dream of love, in every embrace, Hands that speak of hope, in each squeeze, that tell a love story, in each union.
They are the voice of a future that is announced, the dialogue of two souls that is pronounced.
"Hands that join," proclaims the poet, "they are the union that challenges our love. Your link, the promise of a tomorrow, your warmth, the star that wins in my sky."
In the awakening of two hands that wait, a love is revealed that surpasses the shadows.
Hands that are the refuge, the passion, the hope, the universal language, the purest praise.

VIII

I Am the Fire, I am the fire the divine spark, the eternal flame that germinates in the soul.
I am the ardor that dwells in the spirit, the heat that beats in the heart.
I am the fire that illuminates the darkness, that gives life to the truth in its clarity. The light that guides the lost, the beacon that illuminates the paths.
"I am the fire," proclaims the wise, "the knowledge that is not a grievance. My flames, the words of wisdom, my heat, the passion that guides every day."
I am the fire that purifies the being, that transforms pain, without fainting. The crucible that melts fear and rancor, the strength that forges a new love.
"I am the fire," prays the saint, "the spirit that raises the song. My embers, the prayer that rises, my glow, the faith that never denies."
I am the fire that ignites passion, that awakens desire without condition. The heat that is felt on the skin, the spark that lights up in the kiss.
"I am the fire," sighs the lover, "the caress that seeks the moment. My flames, the embrace that envelops, my glow, the love that is revealed."
I am the fire that transforms destiny, that writes in the stars the path.
The power that changes history, the energy that creates memory.
"I am the fire," proclaims the poet, "the inspiration that challenges the mind. My sparks, the muse that inspires, my flame, the voice that never withdraws."
At the altar of life, I am the fire, the element that in the universe I play.
I am the refuge, the passion, the guide, the universal language, poetry.
I am the fire, the unbreakable passion, the energy that in every heart is palpable. I am the vigor that persists in the soul, the brightness that exists in the gaze.

I am the fire that inspires artists, that in each work, lists its flames. The spark that ignites creativity, the impetus that gives life to the city.
"I am the fire," sings the musician, "the melody that in the air is mystical.
My notes, the flames of the song, my rhythm, the dance of passion."
I am the fire that connects spirits, that in unity, finds its limits. The heat that unites soul mates, the flame that in love never freezes.
"I am the fire," unites the lover, "the bond that enchants everyone. My arms, the embrace that protects, my essence, the love that is given."
I am the fire that renews every day, that brings hope, that guides life. The sun that at dawn, paints a new destiny, the star that in the night, inks the path.
"I am the fire," reborn the phoenix, "the strength that from the ashes fixes. My wings, the flight towards the light, my resurgence, the path that seduces."
In the heart of the world, I am the fire, the symbol of a love that is not blind. I am the refuge, the passion, the rebirth, the universal language, the power to be.
I am the fire, the immortal essence, the passion that in the infinite is vital.
I am the embrace that resonates in the void, the echo of a love that always fills.
I am the fire that defies eternity, that in each spark, awakens reality. The flame that burns beyond time, the heat that is felt in the firmament.
"I am the fire," defies the warrior, "the courage that faces the path. My flames, the fight against darkness, my glow, the victory of clarity."
I am the fire that is pure and true love, that in each soul, lights the first star. The love that knows no endings, the passion that transcends mortals.

"I am the fire," loves the eternal, "the feeling that is winter and summer. My embers, the heat of an ageless love, my light, the guide to happiness."
I am the fire that is life in every breath, that in each spark, teaches to love. The life that sprouts from the burnt earth, the existence that by the fire is embraced.
"I am the fire," lives the poet, "the inspiration that challenges life. My sparks, the breath of creation, my ardor, the essence of passion."
In the depth of the cosmos, I am the fire, the dance of the stars, the game. I am the refuge, the passion, the life, the universal language, the fulfilled promise.
I am the fire, the passion that never ceases, the eternal flame that in each being expresses. I am the heat that persists in the cold winter, the glow that insists in the shadow.
I am the fire that guides travelers, that in the night lights up the paths. The light that points the way to follow, the beacon that promises a future.
"I am the fire," guides the explorer, "the hope that in the adventure is the engine. My flames, the map of a world to discover, my glow, the certainty of a destiny to build."
I am the fire that unites hearts, that in the distance overcomes separations. The heat that melts all coldness, the spark that ignites unity.
"I am the fire," unites the lover, "the bond that enchants everyone. My arms, the embrace that protects, my essence, the love that is given."
I am the fire that reveals secrets, that in truth finds its challenges. The flash that illuminates the hidden, the clarity that reveals the result.
"I am the fire," reveals the wise, "the truth that in the mystery is a challenge. My sparks, the key to the unknown, my ardor, the knowledge achieved."
I am the fire that is passion and life, that in each heartbeat is kindled. The strength that drives lovers, the desire that in dreams is constant.

"I am the fire," burns the poet, "the passion that in life challenges. My flames, the impulse of creation, my heat, the essence of inspiration."
In the immensity of the universe, I am the fire, the dance of the flames, the eternal game.

IX

Perhaps, just perhaps, in the twilight of dawn, where dreams still cling to the night, and the stars twinkle their last secrets, a whisper, a desire, a promise of something more is born.
Perhaps, in the sigh of the morning breeze, where the dew kisses each petal with passion, and the horizon is tinged with crimson hopes, the truth that the heart longs to hear is hidden.
Just maybe, in the echo of an "I love you," that slides softly, fearful and sincere, among the folds of time and distance, the refuge, the warmth, the constancy is found.
Perhaps, in the gaze that gets lost in the distance, where longing and tenderness intertwine, and each heartbeat is a dedicated verse, the path to the unexpected is revealed.
Just maybe, in the touch of two souls, that in their dance forget the world and its dramas, and in an instant of unbridled passion, they discover that love is the only dwelling.
Perhaps, in the silence that follows the word, where the purest feeling does not end, and in the calm that envelops the loved one, the future is glimpsed, together, side by side.
Just maybe,
in the embrace that lasts, where strength and tenderness merge, and in each gesture, in each small attention, the story of an eternal devotion is cultivated.
Perhaps, just perhaps, at the end of this poem, where the ink dries and the voice barely burns, the echo of a perhaps, deep and passionate, a long journey to the soul, a destination without end remains.

And perhaps, in the whisper of the night that envelops us, where the shadows dance to the rhythm of desire, and the moon, confidante, keeps our secrets, a bond is forged that not even time dissolves.

Just maybe, in the caress that eternalizes, where the confines of the soul are explored, and each touch is an unspoken word, a universe of calm is discovered.

Perhaps, in the ardor of two hearts on fire, where passion becomes art, and each kiss is a brush that colors life, a story is painted that never departs.

Just maybe, in the promise of a tomorrow, where dreams dress up as reality, and each dawn is a new chapter, the destiny is written with sincerity.

Perhaps, in the reflection of two gazes that meet, where the future is read in an instant, and each gesture is a recited poem, a love that is constant is found.

Just maybe, in the embrace that protects us, where the pulse of eternity is felt, and in each shared heartbeat, in each sigh, life is celebrated with intensity.

Perhaps, just perhaps, in the melody that resonates, where music is the language of feeling, and each note is a step to heaven, the peak of existence may be reached.

And perhaps, in the quiet of a world that awakens, where each breath is a blank canvas, and life unfolds like a star map, routes that destiny has not yet marked may be traced.

Just maybe, in the fusion of two essences, where the alchemy of love is discovered, and each encounter is a discovery, a treasure that shines with fervor may be found.

Perhaps, in the strength of a silent commitment, where words are superfluous and actions speak, and each sacrifice is a precious jewel, a castle that time does not wear down may be built.

Just maybe, in the unconditional surrender, where everything is given without expecting anything in return, and each act of generosity is a shooting star, a path that leads to paradise step by step may be illuminated.

Perhaps, in the passion of an infinite instant, where the clock stops and the world falls silent, and each gaze is a universe in expansion, a romance that resonates like a legend may be lived.

Just maybe, in the promise of a forever, where the future is a garden of possibilities, and each shared dream blooms with vigor, a love that endures in history may be cultivated.

Perhaps, just perhaps, at the end of this verse, where the pen rests and the soul expresses itself, the certainty of a perhaps turned into certainty may remain, a deep love, passionate, and eternal.

And perhaps, in the melody that the wind carries, where the notes rise like waves in the sea, and each chord is a whisper of the earth, a song that can caress the soul may be sung.

Just maybe, in the depth of a gaze, where the mysteries of being are hidden, and each sparkle is an untold story, the book of a past that is reborn may be read.

Perhaps, in the passion of a hug that does not let go, where two fires merge into one, and each heartbeat is a flame that kindles, the warmth of a love that envelops everything may be felt.

Just maybe, in the promise of a whisper, where words become legend, and each phrase is an eternal vow, a pact that not even time takes away may be forged.

Perhaps, in the eternity of a shared instant, where the now is all that matters, and each second is a discovered treasure, the fullness of an endless present may be lived.

Just maybe, in the sincerity of a gesture, where the truth is shown without adornments, and each act is a declaration of intentions, the essence of a pure feeling may be found.

Perhaps, just perhaps, in the infinity of this poem, where words flow like a river to the sea, the resonance of a perhaps that becomes certainty may remain.

And perhaps, in the cadence of a verse that does not end, where each word is a thread in the tapestry of destiny, and poetry becomes the language of the soul, a story that nests in the heart may be woven.

Just maybe, in the promise of a dawn together, where the rising sun brings comfort to the dark night, and each ray of light is a caress that awakens, peace may be found in a reassuring embrace.

Perhaps, in the passion of an endless encounter, where bodies speak without saying a word, and each gesture is a confession of true love, a feeling that encompasses everything may be discovered.

Just maybe, in the eternity of an instant, where time surrenders to the magnitude of the feeling, and each second is an expanding universe, love may be lived in its purest element.

Perhaps, in the depth of an 'I love you' without voice, where silence is the echo of a heart that beats strongly, and each beat is a song to life that is renewed, the power of a love that defies death may be felt.

Just maybe, in the infinity of this poem, where words are stars in the firmament, the trace of a perhaps that becomes forever may remain.

X

In the silence of the night, the owl observes, with eyes that penetrate the darkness and the fog, guardian of ancestral secrets, wise and eternal, its song is a mantra, an echo in time.
The owl, solitary on its sacred branch, sees beyond the shadows, its gaze is winged, knows the mysteries that the world hides, and in its silent flight, the truth responds.
Spirit of the forest, messenger of the divine, its wings unfold messages of destiny, in its presence, the veil is lifted, and the soul listens to what the heart travels.
Under the moon, the owl begins its dance, each movement is a prayer, a hope, in its flight there is passion, there is a fire that burns, it is the free spirit that is kept in the sky.
With each turn, the owl traces a perfect circle, a symbol of unity, of the sacred and the correct, its voice is a call to introspection, a spiritual awakening, a deep connection.
The owl, on its throne of branches and stars, is the bridge between worlds, between eras and sparks, its wisdom is a river that flows incessantly, a deep love that can embrace everything.
In the stillness, the owl is the guardian of the temple, the one who sees the invisible, the one who knows the example, its presence is a touch of the immortal, a passionate being that can love the universe.
And so, the owl, in its nocturnal and divine flight, is the poet of the sky, of destiny and the path, its poem is a song to life and passion, a spiritual hymn that resonates in the heart.

In the vastness of the sky, the owl spreads its wings, like a celestial messenger in the night that does not silence, its eyes, beacons of light.

And perhaps, in the melody that the wind carries, where the notes rise like waves in the sea, and each chord is a whisper of the earth, a song that can caress the soul may be sung.
Just maybe, in the depth of a gaze, where the mysteries of being are hidden, and each sparkle is an untold story, the book of a past that is reborn may be read.
Perhaps, in the passion of a hug that does not let go, where two fires merge into one, and each heartbeat is a flame that kindles, the warmth of a love that envelops everything may be felt.
Just maybe, in the promise of a whisper, where words become legend, and each phrase is an eternal vow, a pact that not even time takes away may be forged.
Perhaps, in the eternity of a shared instant, where the now is all that matters, and each second is a discovered treasure, the fullness of an endless present may be lived.
Just maybe, in the sincerity of a gesture, where the truth is shown without adornments, and each act is a declaration of intentions, the essence of a pure feeling may be found.
Perhaps, just perhaps, in the infinity of this poem, where words flow like a river to the sea, the resonance of a perhaps that becomes certainty may remain.
And perhaps, in the cadence of a verse that does not end, where each word is a thread in the tapestry of destiny, and poetry becomes the language of the soul, a story that nests in the heart may be woven.
Just maybe, in the promise of a dawn together, where the rising sun brings comfort to the dark night, and each ray of light is a caress that awakens, peace may be found in a reassuring embrace.

Perhaps, in the passion of an endless encounter, where bodies speak without saying a word, and each gesture is a confession of true love, a feeling that encompasses everything may be discovered.

Just maybe, in the eternity of an instant, where time surrenders to the magnitude of the feeling, and each second is an expanding universe, love may be lived in its purest element.

Perhaps, in the depth of an 'I love you' without voice, where silence is the echo of a heart that beats strongly, and each beat is a song to life that is renewed, the power of a love that defies death may be felt.

Just maybe, in the infinity of this poem, where words are stars in the firmament, the trace of a perhaps that becomes forever may remain.

In the twilight of the forest, the owl flies without hurry, with the moon as a guide, there is a breeze in its gaze, it is the master of silence, the oracle of the night, its flight is a ritual, a sacred waste.

The owl, with its song, weaves the fabric of destiny, in each note there is a destiny, a divine path, it is the guardian of dreams, the custodian of faith, in its presence, the spirit rises, stands up.

With eyes that see beyond flesh and bone, the owl understands pain, love, weight, it is the comfort for the soul that seeks light, in its wisdom, there is a refuge, a sweet lullaby.

In the flight of the owl there is an ancestral dance, each flap is a verse, a spiritual song, it is the passion of the earth that wants to reach the sky, in its gaze, there is a fire that cannot be extinguished.

The owl, on its throne of air, of leaves and sky, is the poet of the eternal, of mystery and longing, its poem is a river that flows in the soul, a deep love, spiritual, that calms everything.

And so, the owl, in its flight, is the poet of the sacred, the one who sings to life, to immaculate love, its poem is a song to passion and devotion, a spiritual hymn that unites us in a single prayer.

XI

At the top of the world, where silence speaks, the owl, wise and solitary, balsams in the night. With full moon eyes and a plumage woven of shadows, it prepares for flight, chosen by destiny.
Under the starry mantle, the transformation begins, the owl sheds its mystical condition. Its wings expand, its spirit rises, and in a sigh of the wind, its being is renewed.
Now it is a condor, majestic and powerful, with wings that touch the skies, free and glorious. It soars the heights with overflowing passion, each beat is a verse, each flight is vibrant.
The condor, king of the Andes, spirit of the mountain, in its flight there is a song that the earth accompanies. It is the guardian of the skies, the messenger of the sun, in its gaze there is a fire that was never seen.
With each turn in the air, the condor draws life, its dance is a prayer, a fulfilled promise. It is the embrace of the wind, the caress of the sky, a passionate being that flies without fear.
The condor, in its ascent, touches the face of God, and in that sacred moment, time stops at its voice. It is the bridge between the earth and the infinite, a living poem, a blessed spirit.
In the immensity of the blue, the condor is the guide, with its flight it teaches us true wisdom. It is the love that rises above the storm, a spiritual being that accentuates in its greatness.
And so, the owl transforms, its essence is not lost, it becomes a condor, and its poetry extends.

A beautiful being, deep, passionate and spiritual, that in its flight gives us a celestial spectacle.
The condor, in its flight, transcends the firmament, with spread wings, it embraces the wind.
It is the spirit of the mountain, the heart of the sky, in its gaze there is a world, a dream without a veil.
With each flap, the condor writes its history, a tale of freedom, of struggle and glory.

He is the messenger between the gods and men, a bridge of hope between different horizons.
At the top of the world, the condor perches, with the majesty of a flower that unfolds beautifully. He is the guardian of wisdom, the bearer of truth, in his flight there is a message of unity and kindness. The condor, with his song, invokes the ancestors, and in his sacred dance, celebrates the mysteries. He is the love that ascends above the clouds, a spiritual being that does not hide in his greatness. The condor, lord of the air, on his celestial throne, with his wings spread, commits himself to the wind.
He is the spirit of the peaks, the soul of the height, in his flight there is a prayer, a sacred adventure.

With each powerful beat, the condor defies gravity, a ballet of strength and grace, a spectacle of freedom. He is the messenger of the sky, the herald of open spaces, a bridge between the earthly and the still uncertain mysteries.
At the summit of the Andes, the condor stops to rest, with the majesty of a king, with the peace of an altar.
He is the guardian of creation, the custodian of life, in his gaze there is a reflection, a flame never defeated.
The condor, with his song, invokes the essence of being, and in his sacred dance, invites us to be reborn. He is the love that rises, that

overcomes every storm, a spiritual being that encourages us in his flight.

The condor, emperor of the ether, perches on his throne of clouds, with the dignity of the centuries and the wisdom of the roses. He is the spirit of the Andes, the whisper of the earth, in his flight there is a poem, a revelation that is banished.

With each beat of wings, the condor tears the veil of time, a ritual of strength and mystery, a song to the wind. He is the messenger of the eternal, the custodian of celestial secrets, a bridge between the divine and earthly desires.

At the summit of existence, the condor contemplates the infinite, with the serenity of a monk, with the fervor of a rite. He is the guardian of memory, the bearer of vision, in his gaze there is a universe, an immense song.

The condor, with his flight, invokes the depth of the soul, and in his sacred dance, reveals calm. He is the love that rises, that touches the essence of life, a spiritual being that invites us in his flight.

XII

In the depth of your eyes, a universe unfolds, with looks that are
poems, and each blink a surrender.
They are two oceans of mystery, two suns in the dark night, in them
life is reflected, the purest passion.
Your eyes, mirrors of the soul, windows to the unfathomable, in their
abyss hide stories, ineffable truths. They are the refuge of your dreams,
the altar of your secrets, in their depth, the most perfect moments are
woven.
With each look, you reveal a cosmos of emotions, a fabric of feelings, a
kaleidoscope of visions.
Your eyes are two living flames, two beacons that guide, in their depth,
the heat that never cools is felt.
In the intensity of your eyes, there is a fire that does not go out, a
passion that burns, that is not daunted by anything. They are two
precious jewels, two gems without equal, in their depth, an immortal
love is found.

Your eyes, two poems written on the canvas of time, two endless
stories, two promises of wind. In their depth, the infinite is discovered,
an intense, passionate love, an exquisite feeling.
And so, in the depth of your eyes, the whole is found, a universe of
sensations, a never silent sea. They are two worlds to explore, two
lights in eternity, in their depth, the most beautiful reality is lived.
With the depth of my eyes a story without age is told, a story that in
the silence of a look can be heard.

They are two abysses where the soul plunges, seeking the truth, in them the universe is reflected, in a blink you can dream.
With the depth of my eyes a starry sky is painted, a canvas of desires and memories, of an illuminated past. They are two flames that burn with passion, with an uncontrolled fire, in their brightness is found strength, an unbroken spirit.
With the depth of my eyes the darkest secrets are unveiled, the doors to dreams are opened, the purest bonds are unleashed. They are two seas of hope, where secure feelings sail, in their waves life is rocked, with their tides of futures.
With the depth of my eyes a network of infinite possibilities is woven, a framework of paths and choices, of eternal realities.
They are two mirrors that reflect the soul, with all its complexities, in their gaze love is discovered, with all its intensities.
With the depth of my eyes a poem without end is written, an ode to existence, to each vital moment. They are two stars that guide in the darkness, with their celestial light, in their depth is found the essence, a spiritual bond.
With the depth of my eyes the enigmas of being are shelled, each look is a labyrinth, where feelings can bloom.
They are two guardians of the internal fire, two torches in the twilight, in their brightness the passion is glimpsed, a love that never fades.
With the depth of my eyes epics of love and pain are narrated, stories that time cannot erase, nor the strongest heartbreak.
They are two beacons in the storm, two refuges in adversity, in their light strength is forged, sincerity is cultivated.
With the depth of my eyes the codes of the soul are deciphered, each sparkle is a key, a door to calm.
They are two parallel universes, two cosmos in constant expansion, in their infinite is found the essence, the purest connection.
With the depth of my eyes the pulse of creation is felt, a rhythm that beats with the universe, in perfect synchronization.

They are two living poems, two songs that the wind will carry, in their melody life is intoned, a symphony that will always be.
With the depth of my eyes a whirlwind of sensations is unleashed,

A whirlwind of emotions, a swirl of passions.
They are two wild oceans, two seas that know no end, in their waves the destiny is navigated, the end is discovered.
With the depth of my eyes the confines of being are explored, where each look is a journey to the most recondite of wanting.
They are two spheres of mystery, two keys to the unexplored, in their abyss love is found, in their reflection the sacred.
With the depth of my eyes the veils of feeling unfold, each blink is a chapter, a story to discover. They are two twin flames, burning with constant fervor, in their light the desire is revealed, a burning and vibrant fire.
With the depth of my eyes the threads of destiny intertwine, weaving a network of dreams, a fine and divine tapestry. They are two stars in the cosmos, two guides in the darkness, in their brightness the passion is found, the purest clarity.
With the depth of my eyes the secrets of the soul are whispered, each sparkle is a word, a balm that soothes.
They are two sources of life, from where the essence springs, in their depth the pulse is felt, the most intense presence.
With the depth of my eyes eternity is lived in an instant, a suspended moment, a giant feeling.
They are two doors to infinity, two promises of immortality, in their gaze the history is forged, a legacy of depth.
With the depth of my eyes the secrets of the universe unfold, each wink is a constellation, a diverse destiny. They are two jewels that keep the reflection of the stars, in their brightness the story is told, a beautiful and sincere saga.

With the depth of my eyes the flames of desire are ignited, each look is a hug, a feeling that has no remedy.
They are two beacons that illuminate the path of the heart, in their light the passion is discovered, a fire without condition.
With the depth of my eyes the seas of emotion are navigated, each tear is a river, a flow of devotion. They are two safe ports in the storm of life, in their calm love is found, a promise always fulfilled.
With the depth of my eyes the dreams of the night are forged, each blink is a desire, a flight that sheds reproach.
They are two guardians of the mystery, two accomplices of fantasy, in their depth magic is lived, a sweet utopia.
With the depth of my eyes the pulse of the world is felt, a beat that resonates with every second.

XIII

When your fingers paint an infinity on my skin, the cosmos is unleashed, an exquisite universe. When your fingers paint an infinity on my skin, each stroke is a desire, a blessed whisper.
When your fingers paint an infinity on my skin, the night lights up, it becomes a rite. When your fingers paint an infinity on my skin, time stops, it surrenders to instinct.
When your fingers paint an infinity on my skin, the stars envy, the sky admits its crime. When your fingers paint an infinity on my skin, passion ignites, it becomes a scream.
When your fingers paint an infinity on my skin, reality fades, it comes into conflict. When your fingers paint an infinity on my skin, love is revealed, pure and explicit.
When your fingers paint an infinity on my skin, the rivers overflow, the sea stirs, it is not a myth. When your fingers paint an infinity on my skin, life makes sense, each moment is a milestone.

When your fingers paint an infinity on my skin, our souls merge, in an infinite embrace. When your fingers paint an infinity on my skin, a poetry is born, an infinite feeling.
When your fingers paint an infinity on my skin, galaxies unfold, in a blessed act. When your fingers paint an infinity on my skin, each caress is a verse, a written feeling.
When your fingers paint an infinity on my skin, the fire of passion becomes a rite. When your fingers paint an infinity on my skin, the art of your love, is inscribed in my being.
When your fingers paint an infinity on my skin, the depth of desire knows no limit or mess. When your fingers paint an infinity on my skin, with each touch the heat, the appetite is felt.
When your fingers paint an infinity on my skin, the intensity of the union is a pure scream. When your fingers paint an infinity on my skin, our worlds merge, into a single myth.
When your fingers paint an infinity on my skin, eternity is captured, in an exquisite bond. When your fingers paint an infinity on my skin, a story is written, an infinite legacy.
When your fingers paint an infinity on my skin, the symphony of touch rises, sublime and blessed. When your fingers paint an infinity on my skin, each contour explored is a rediscovered map.
When your fingers paint an infinity on my skin, the senses awaken, a feast of sensations. When your fingers paint an infinity on my skin, the fabric of our story is embroidered in each gesture.
When your fingers paint an infinity on my skin, the canvas of existence is colored with passion. When your fingers paint an infinity on my skin, words are superfluous, for the language of the heart speaks.
When your fingers paint an infinity on my skin, passion overflows, a raging and cursed river. When your fingers paint an infinity on my skin, each touch is a lightning bolt, a love never omitted.

When your fingers paint an infinity on my skin, desire incarnates, a fervor never written. When your fingers paint an infinity on my skin, the intensity consumes us, an unrestricted fire.

When your fingers paint an infinity on my skin, souls merge, a shared destiny. When your fingers paint an infinity on my skin, ecstasy is reached, an indefinite climax.

When your fingers paint an infinity on my skin, emotion intensifies, a feeling not measured. When your fingers paint an infinity on my skin, life is redefined, an unforeseen path.

When your fingers paint an infinity on my skin, the universe conspires, an unwritten pact. When your fingers paint an infinity on my skin, our canvas is eternalized, an undescribed art.

XIV

Cursed sweetness, yours, that floods my being without permission, Cursed sweetness, yours, that makes me a slave to a sigh.
Cursed sweetness, yours, that awakens the dormant fire, Cursed sweetness, yours, that leaves its trace in my soul.
Cursed sweetness, yours, that becomes light among shadows, Cursed sweetness, yours, that seduces and seduces my heart.
Cursed sweetness, yours, that is storm and calm, Cursed sweetness, yours, that is balm and weapon.
Cursed sweetness, yours, that condemns me and saves me, Cursed sweetness, yours, that is carved in every verse.
Cursed sweetness, yours, that is poetry on the skin, Cursed sweetness, yours, that makes me yours, faithful.
Cursed sweetness, yours, that entangles my days and nights, Cursed sweetness, yours, that passionately ignites my mind, Cursed sweetness, yours, that is the sweetest wine in my mouth, Cursed sweetness, yours, that lodges in my heart.
Cursed sweetness, yours, that is the melody in my silence, Cursed sweetness, yours, that is the canvas of my dreams. Cursed sweetness, yours, that is the whisper of the wind, Cursed sweetness, yours, that is my only and true breath.
Cursed sweetness, yours, that is the strength that guides me, Cursed sweetness, yours, that is the light of my days. Cursed sweetness, yours, that is the reason for my existence, Cursed sweetness, yours, that teaches me to love without end.

Cursed sweetness, yours, that is the anchor in my storm, Cursed sweetness, yours, that always feeds my soul.
Cursed sweetness, yours, that is the fire in my cold, Cursed sweetness, yours, that is my peace and my delirium.
Cursed sweetness, yours, that is the echo of my voice, Cursed sweetness, yours, that lifts me from the ground to the cross.

Cursed sweetness, yours, that is the eternal oath, Cursed sweetness, yours, that traps me in its winter.
Cursed sweetness, yours, that is the caress in the distance, Cursed sweetness, yours, that offers me its constancy. Cursed sweetness, yours, that is the sigh in the breeze, Cursed sweetness, yours, that eternally eternalizes in my being.
Cursed sweetness, yours, that is the beacon in my darkness, Cursed sweetness, yours, that is the promise of eternity.
Cursed sweetness, yours, that is the song of the sea, Cursed sweetness, yours, that teaches me to fly.

Cursed sweetness, yours, that is the passion that does not go out, Cursed sweetness, yours, that pierces my burning chest.
Cursed sweetness, yours, that is the tie that does not untie, Cursed sweetness, yours, that is the story that never ends.
Cursed sweetness, yours, that is the kiss I always wait for, Cursed sweetness, yours, that is the love I consider most sincere.
Cursed sweetness, yours, that is the strength of my passion, Cursed sweetness, yours, that is the source of my inspiration.
Cursed sweetness, yours, that is the hug in my solitude, Cursed sweetness, yours, that is the truth in my reality.
Cursed sweetness, yours, that is the rhythm of my heart, Cursed sweetness, yours, that is my madness and my reason.

Cursed sweetness, yours, that is the rain in my desert, Cursed sweetness, yours, that is my refuge, my port. Cursed sweetness, yours, that is the heat in my winter, Cursed sweetness, yours, that is my guide, my eternal beacon.
Cursed sweetness, yours, that is the sigh of my soul, Cursed sweetness, yours, that is the calm in my palm.
Cursed sweetness, yours, that is the fire that consumes me, Cursed sweetness, yours, that is the love that assumes.
Cursed sweetness, yours, that is the relief in my sorrow, Cursed sweetness, yours, that is the light that fills me.
Cursed sweetness, yours, that is the air for my fire, Cursed sweetness, yours, that is the dream I pursue.
Cursed sweetness, yours, that is the song of my life, Cursed sweetness, yours, that is the ignited passion.

Cursed sweetness, yours, that is the reflection of my being, Cursed sweetness, yours, that is the love I want to have.
Cursed sweetness, yours, that is the journey without end, Cursed sweetness, yours, that is the port and the storm.
Cursed sweetness, yours, that is the promise in my ear, Cursed sweetness, yours, that is the hidden treasure.
Cursed sweetness, yours, that is the comfort in my crying, Cursed sweetness, yours, that is my holiest secret.
Cursed sweetness, yours, that is the passion that guides me, Cursed sweetness, yours, that is the poetry of every day.
Cursed sweetness, yours, that is the dawn in my night, Cursed sweetness, yours, that is the whisper that reproaches me.
Cursed sweetness, yours, that is the flame in my candle, Cursed sweetness, yours, that is the most beautiful story.
Cursed sweetness, yours, that is the wind in my sail, Cursed sweetness, yours, that is the force that reveals. Cursed sweetness, yours, that is the path I follow, Cursed sweetness, yours, that is the shelter I pursue.

XV

The greatness that presides over me, is the strength of my burning spirit, The greatness that presides over me, is the love that beats constantly and fervently.
The greatness that presides over me, is the passion that ignites in my chest, The greatness that presides over me, is the hope that extends in the darkness.
The greatness that presides over me, is the courage that never gives up, The greatness that presides over me, is the truth that always finds itself and does not hide.
The greatness that presides over me, is the desire that is written in the stars, The greatness that presides over me, is the destiny that is inscribed in my soul.
The greatness that presides over me, is the fire that perpetuates in my being, The greatness that presides over me, is the life that always continues.
The greatness that presides over me, is the dream that is never abandoned,
The greatness that presides over me, is the voice that resounds and intones in the wind.
The greatness that presides over me, is the strength that rises in adversity, The greatness that presides over me, is the faith that is planted in my heart.
The greatness that presides over me, is the art that paints on the canvas of life, The greatness that presides over me, is the history that reinvents itself every day.

The greatness that presides over me, is the echo of my existence, The greatness that presides over me, is the essence of my consciousness. The greatness that presides over me, is the hug that the world gives me, The greatness that presides over me, is the passion that never goes away.

The greatness that presides over me, is the impulse that makes me create, The greatness that presides over me, is the path that invites me to walk.

The greatness that presides over me, is the light that guides my path, The greatness that presides over me, is love, my only and true treasure.

The greatness that presides over me, is the strength that makes me fight, The greatness that presides over me, is the will to never give up. The greatness that presides over me, is the value that makes me dream, The greatness that presides over me, is the promise to always love. The greatness that presides over me, is the whisper of the starry night, The greatness that presides over me, is the caress of the dawn.

The greatness that presides over me, is the fire that burns in my soul, The greatness that presides over me, is the love that is kept in my heart. The greatness that presides over me, is the inspiration of each verse, The greatness that presides over me, is the universe in a kiss.

The greatness that presides over me, is the passion that is not measured, The greatness that presides over me, is the dream that nests in reality.

The greatness that presides over me, is the strength of the tides, The greatness that presides over me, is the hope that does not despair. The greatness that presides over me, is the value in the battle, The greatness that presides over me, is the light that does not fail in the darkness.

The greatness that presides over me, is the enigma of eternity, The greatness that presides over me, is the complexity in its simplicity. The greatness that presides over me, is the symphony of the cosmos, The greatness that presides over me, is the infinite in the atoms.

The greatness that presides over me, is the depth of thought, The greatness that presides over me, is the mystery of the firmament. The greatness that presides over me, is the passion that is inscribed in time, The greatness that presides over me, is the masterpiece that the universe describes.
The greatness that presides over me, is the fabric of reality, The greatness that presides over me, is beauty in its purest truth. The greatness that presides over me, is the legacy of history, The greatness that presides over me, is the triumph, the memory. The greatness that presides over me, is the labyrinth of existence, The greatness that presides over me, is the essence of resistance.

The greatness that presides over me, is the art that challenges, The greatness that presides over me, is the poetry that nests in the soul. The greatness that presides over me, is the sigh of the centuries, The greatness that presides over me, is the challenge to dangers. The greatness that presides over me, is the dance of the galaxies, The greatness that presides over me, is the union of ecstatic souls. The greatness that presides over me, is the voice of the ancestors, The greatness that presides over me, is the legacy of the masters. The greatness that presides over me, is the mystery without resolution, The greatness that presides over me, is the love that can conquer all. The greatness that presides over me, is the wisdom of the earth, The greatness that presides over me, is the beauty that is discovered and clings.
The greatness that presides over me, is the power of creation, The greatness that presides over me, is the passion that gives life to the song.
The greatness that presides over me, is the journey through time, The greatness that presides over me, is the encounter with the wind. The greatness that presides over me, is the flame that never extinguishes,

The greatness that presides over me, is the history that always distinguishes itself.
The greatness that presides over me, is the reflection of the moon in the sea,
The greatness that presides over me, is the desire to never cease. The greatness that presides over me, is the art of knowing how to live,
The greatness that presides over me, is the passion that drives me to continue.
The greatness that presides over me, is the wisdom of the centuries, The greatness that presides over me, is the courage in the face of dangers.
The greatness that presides over me, is the melody of life, The greatness that presides over me, is the strength that is never forgotten.
The greatness that presides over me, is the mystery of the unknown, The greatness that presides over me, is the path that I have always traveled.
The greatness that presides over me, is the promise of a new day,
The greatness that presides over me, is the hope that nests in my chest.

XVI

I remember you and I said goodbye to you badly, in that broken silence, I remember you and I said goodbye to you badly, with a torn soul.
I remember you and I said goodbye to you badly, among hidden tears, I remember you and I said goodbye to you badly, leaving our lives behind.
I remember you and I said goodbye to you badly, with an unspoken goodbye, I remember you and I said goodbye to you badly, in a drowned whisper. I remember you and I said goodbye to you badly, with my heart in my hand, I remember you and I said goodbye to you badly, in a distant destiny.
I remember you and I said goodbye to you badly, with unfulfilled promises, I remember you and I said goodbye to you badly, in the parted farewells.
I remember you and I said goodbye to you badly, with love still burning, I remember you and I said goodbye to you badly, and now I think of you eternally. I remember you and I said goodbye to you badly, with the wind that carries my words, I remember you and I said goodbye to you badly, in the nights full of shadows.

I remember you and I said goodbye to you badly, with the hope of a reunion, I remember you and I said goodbye to you badly, searching for our center in time.
I remember you and I said goodbye to you badly, with the passion that still calls us, I remember you and I said goodbye to you badly, with the flame that inflames the soul.
I remember you and I said goodbye to you badly, with the pain of a love that persists, I remember you and I said goodbye to you badly, with the certainty that you still exist.

I remember you and I said goodbye to you badly, with the melancholy that invades me, I remember you and I said goodbye to you badly, in the quietness that my soul evades.

I remember you and I said goodbye to you badly, with the echo of your voice that resounds, I remember you and I said goodbye to you badly, in the sadness that like fog is entrusted.

I remember you and I said goodbye to you badly, with the strength of an unforgotten love, I remember you and I said goodbye to you badly, in the memory that remains by my side.

I remember you and I said goodbye to you badly, with the passion that still unites us, I remember you and I said goodbye to you badly, in the hope that flows like a river.

I remember you and I said goodbye to you badly, with the story still to be written, I remember you and I said goodbye to you badly, with the soul that does not know how to lie.

I remember you and I said goodbye to you badly, with the love that still beats strong, I remember you and I said goodbye to you badly, with the hope of seeing you.

I remember you and I said goodbye to you badly, with the passion that does not go out, I remember you and I said goodbye to you badly, with the wound that still burdens me.

I remember you and I said goodbye to you badly, with the desire to start over, I remember you and I said goodbye to you badly, with the certainty that I am going to love you.

I remember you and I said goodbye to you badly, in the plot of our intertwined destiny, I remember you and I said goodbye to you badly, in the labyrinth of a love without aim.

I remember you and I said goodbye to you badly, with the intensity of a deep ocean, I remember you and I said goodbye to you badly, with the complexity of a round feeling.

I remember you and I said goodbye to you badly, in the paradox of our separation, I remember you and I said goodbye to you badly, in the duality of passion and reason.
I remember you and I said goodbye to you badly, in the enigma of what could have been, I remember you and I said goodbye to you badly, in the mystery of what is still to be seen.
I remember you and I said goodbye to you badly, in the symphony of an unwanted goodbye, I remember you and I said goodbye to you badly, in the echo of an undefeated love.
I remember you and I said goodbye to you badly, in the search for a new dawn, I remember you and I said goodbye to you badly, in the hope of one day being reborn again.

I remember you and I said goodbye to you badly, in the depth of each shooting star, I remember you and I said goodbye to you badly, in the reflection of a love that never fades.

I remember you and I said goodbye to you badly, in the dance of the rain on the glass, I remember you and I said goodbye to you badly, in the whisper of the wind that does not know how to be silent.

I remember you and I said goodbye to you badly, in the passion that hides in the shadows, I remember you and I said goodbye to you badly, in the desire that responds in my chest.

I remember you and I said goodbye to you badly, in the memory that is lost in time, I remember you and I said goodbye to you badly, in the hope that lights up in my soul.

I remember you and I said goodbye to you badly, in the whirlwind of an uncontrollable desire, I remember you and I said goodbye to you badly, with the strength of an irrepressible hurricane.

I remember you and I said goodbye to you badly, in the passion that spreads like fire, I remember you and I said goodbye to you badly, in the complexity of a love that never goes out.

I remember you and I said goodbye to you badly, in the labyrinth of emotions that intersect, I remember you and I said goodbye to you badly, in the storm of feelings that embrace us.

I remember you and I said goodbye to you badly, in the heat of a memory that does not fade, I remember you and I said goodbye to you badly, in the intensity of a love that always grows.

I remember you and I said goodbye to you badly, in the depth of a soul that tears, I remember you and I said goodbye to you badly, in the passion that ties like an overflowing river.

I remember you and I said goodbye to you badly, in the fusion of two beings that long for each other, I remember you and I said goodbye to you badly, in the eternity of two hearts that watch over each other.

I remember you and I said goodbye to you badly, in the passion of a goodbye that still burns, I remember you and I said goodbye to you badly, in the wound that time does not repair.
I remember you and I said goodbye to you badly, in the struggle of a love that clings, I remember you and I said goodbye to you badly, in the hope that declares itself in the night.
I remember you and I said goodbye to you badly, in the fire of a persistent memory, I remember you and I said goodbye to you badly, in the strength of an impatient feeling.
I remember you and I said goodbye to you badly, in the complexity of our united souls, I remember you and I said goodbye to you badly, in the passion of our shared lives.

XVII

On the edge of night and dawn, where dreams and reality intertwine,
Balance is the fire that does not cease, the passion that unleashes in the
wind, is the whisper of nature, that in the silence of the night narrates.
It is the pulse that throbs in the storm, the light that stands out among
shadows, is the courage that stirs in fear, and in every challenge,
unpacks strength.
In the center of this cosmos in motion, where destiny weaves its lace,
balance is more than a feeling, it is the art of living with courage.
Thus, with words that the heart incites, I seek emotion in its purest
state, like the poet who gets excited in the struggle, and finds in
balance his secure future.
On the canvas of the sky, the dawn awakens, with brushstrokes of light
that adorn the horizon, and in that sacred moment, passion awakens,
like a volcano that forms in the poet's chest.
Balance is the dance between night and day, the eternal embrace of the
moon and the sun, is the melody that is sent in the wind, a hymn of
life that plays the harp of the soul with love.
It is the strength that is heard in silence, the tightrope walker who
sways on the rope of destiny, is the passion that nests and fights in the
heart, and in each verse, like a phoenix, is reborn and grows.
In the symphony of this vibrant universe, where each star is a verse in
eternity, balance is the resonant bridge, that unites dreams with reality.
Thus, with each word that the spirit elevates, I seek passion in its most
faithful expression, like the poet who dares in passion, to paint his
destiny in the sky with a brush.

In the vastness of the cosmos, where love is gestated, where each star is a beat, a sigh of the night, there the poem is woven, with passion that never subtracts, a song that in the deep soul is stripped.

Balance is the ardor of two souls that meet, the collision of two universes in a kiss, is the eternal promise that lovers tell each other, in the silence where everything is confessed.

It is the passion that is revealed in the breeze, the desire that ignites in the gaze, is the measureless delivery, pure and beautiful, that extends in the embrace of the night.

In the theater of this world, where every act is art, where passion is the script and the heart the actor, balance is the masterpiece, part by part, of the purest love.

Thus, with verses that passion dictates and aligns, I seek depth in its most sincere form, like the poet who fine-tunes in love, and in balance finds the light he waits for.

In the abyss of passion, where the fire rises, where each spark is a desire, a caress of destiny, there the poem is sung, with fervor that never tires, an echo that nests in the heart, pure and divine.

Balance is the whisper of two souls in the dance, the sway of life in a shared sigh, is the story that is launched with each beat, in the silence where secrets are born.

It is the passion that submerges in the ocean, the wave that rises in the storm, is the strength that emerges in love, and in each wave, like a song, enchants.

On the canvas of this world, where every color is emotion, where passion is the brush and the soul the canvas, balance is the painting, the sublime creation, that is revealed with the touch of the most intense feeling.

Thus, with rhymes that passion weaves and intertwines, I seek the essence in its most truthful manifestation, like the poet who embraces in love, and in balance finds the star he most expects.

XVIII

"I am weak"
whispers the wind at dawn,
"I am weak",
confesses the moon to the sea,
"I am weak",
declares the sun in its dance,
"I am weak",
admits the night when it shines.
"I am weak",
murmurs the river that flows,
"I am weak",
proclaims the tree to the sky,
"I am weak",
sings the flower that includes itself,
"I am weak",
shouts the fire with sleeplessness.

"I am weak",
says the star that twinkles,
"I am weak",
expresses the time that goes by,
"I am weak",
reveals the shadow that oscillates,
"I am weak",
accepts the destiny without more.
"I am weak",
but in my weakness, strong,
"I am weak",
and in my fragility, whole,
"I am weak",
and in my vulnerability, luck,
"I am weak", and in my sincerity, sincere.

"I am weak",
and in that weakness, passion,
"I am weak",
and in that passion, life,
"I am weak",
and in that life, a lesson,
"I am weak",
and in that lesson, exit.
"I am weak",
and in that exit, encounter,
"I am weak",
and in that encounter, love,
"I am weak",
and in that love, center,
"I am weak", and in that center, ardor.
"I am weak",
and in that ardor, poetry,
"I am weak",
and in that poetry, art,
"I am weak",
and in that art, melody,
"I am weak", and in that melody, part.
"I am weak",
and in that part, everything,
"I am weak",
and in that everything, nothing,
"I am weak", and in that nothing, mud,
"I am weak", and in that mud, winged.
"I am weak",
and in that wing, flight,
"I am weak",
and in that flight, sky,

"I am weak",
and in that sky, longing,
"I am weak",
and in that longing, comfort.
"I am weak",
and in that comfort, strength,
"I am weak",
and in that strength, grow,
"I am weak",
and in that growth, certainty,
"I am weak",
and in that certainty, being.
"I am weak",
and in that being, infinite,
"I am weak",
and in that infinite, eternal,
"I am weak",
and in that eternal, myth,
"I am weak",
and in that myth, winter.
"I am weak",
and in that winter, spring,
"I am weak",
and in that spring, flower,
"I am weak",
and in that flower, the wait,
"I am weak", and in that wait, color.
"I am weak",
and in that color, white,
"I am weak",
and in that white, purity,
"I am weak",

and in that purity,
I start, "I am weak",
and in that start, nature.
"I am weak",
and in that nature, life,
" I am weak",
and in that life, passion,
"I am weak",
and in that passion, wound,
"I am weak",
and in that wound, song.
"I am weak",
and in that song, history,
"I am weak",
and in that history, memory,
"I am weak",
and in that memory, glory,
"I am weak",
and in that glory, victory.

"I am weak",
and in that victory, peace,
"I am weak",
and in that peace, beginning,
"I am weak",
and in that beginning, capable,
"I am weak",
and in that capable, effort.
"I am weak",
and in that effort, path,
"I am weak",
and in that path, destiny,

"I am weak",
and in that destiny, divine,
"I am weak",
and in that divine, fine.
"I am weak",
and in that fine, detail,
"I am weak",
and in that detail, greatness,
"I am weak",
and in that greatness, dance,
"I am weak", and in that dance, beauty.
"I am weak",
and in that beauty, light,
"I am weak",
and in that light, hope,
"I am weak",
and in that hope, cross,
"I am weak",
and in that cross, balance.
"I am weak",
and in that balance, equilibrium,
"I am weak",
and in that equilibrium, truth,
"I am weak",
and in that truth, delirium,
"I am weak", and in that delirium, freedom.
"I am weak",
and in that freedom, flight,
"I am weak",
and in that flight, dream,
"I am weak",
and in that dream, longing,

"I am weak",
and in that longing, owner.
"I am weak",
and in that owner, mystery,
"I am weak",
and in that mystery, discovery,
"I am weak",
and in that discovery, empire,
"I am weak",
and in that empire, feeling.
"I am weak",
and in that feeling, deep,
"I am weak",
and in that deep, universe,
"I am weak",
and in that universe, second,
"I am weak", and in that second, verse.
"I am weak",
and in that verse, word,
"I am weak",
and in that word, power,
"I am weak",
and in that power, praise,
"I am weak",
and in that praise, knowledge.
"I am weak",
and in that knowledge, understanding,
"I am weak",
and in that understanding, key,
"I am weak",
and in that key, feeling,
"I am weak",

and in that feeling, bird.
"I am weak",
and in that bird, flight,
"I am weak",
and in that flight, freedom,
"I am weak",
and in that freedom, duel,
"I am weak",
and in that duel, city.
"I am weak",
"I am weak",
and in that city, street,
"I am weak",
and in that street, step,
"I am weak",
and in that step, valley,
"I am weak",
and in that valley, sunset.
"I am weak"
and in that sunset, dawn,
"I am weak",
and in that dawn, day,
"I am weak",
and in that day, grow,
"I am weak",
and in that growth, joy.
"I am weak",
and in that joy, laughter,
"I am weak",
and in that laughter, guffaw,
"I am weak",
and in that guffaw, breeze,

"I am weak",
and in that breeze, dawn.
"I am weak",
and in that dawn, light,
"I am weak",
and in that light, clarity,
"I am weak",
and in that clarity, cross,
"I am weak",
and in that cross, city.
"I am weak",
and in that city, people,
"I am weak",
and in those people, crowd,
"I am weak",
and in that crowd, present,
"I am weak",
and in that present, youth.
"I am weak",
and in that youth, future,
"I am weak",
and in that future, hope,
"I am weak",
and in that hope, wall,
"I am weak",
and in that wall, spear.
"I am weak",
and in that spear, shield,
"I am weak",
and in that shield, protection,
"I am weak",
and in that protection, mute,

"I am weak",
and in that mute, song.
"I am weak",
and in that song, melody,
"I am weak",
and in that melody, sound,
"I am weak",
and in that sound, harmony,
"I am weak",
and in that harmony, sense.
"I am weak",
and in that sense, touch,
"I am weak",
and in that touch, skin,
"I am weak",
and in that skin, contact,
"I am weak",
and in that contact, honey.
"I am weak",
and in that honey, sweetness,
"I am weak",
and in that sweetness, taste,
"I am weak",
and in that taste, madness,
"I am weak",
and in that madness, color.
"I am weak",
and in that color, rainbow,
"I am weak",
and in that rainbow, rain,
"I am weak",
and in that rain, iris,

"I am weak",
and in that iris, test.
"I am weak",
and in that test, challenge.

XIX

In the celestial balance of Libra,
where justice dresses up, where harmony is a whisper that unravels in
the wind, there the poem is forged, with the delicacy of a rose that
does not wither, a song to divine aesthetics, that throbs in the soul of
Libra.
Libra, sign of balance, you inherited the grace of Venus, in your being
intertwine, love and beauty that you never exhausted, you are
diplomacy made flesh, and your touch, a refined art, you make life a
canvas, where each stroke is a painted dream.
You are duality made light, in a single fused existence, peace is your
banner, with a will forged in steel, in you is discovered, the naked
truth, without veil or disguise, and in your balance, the clarity of
justice, its purity brings us.

Your heart is a sanctuary, of equality and compassion, where each emotion is weighed, with meticulous precision, you are the judge of the gods, who without bias or rancor, you seek in each verdict, perfect justice, your greatest honor.

In love you are surrender, with a freedom that knows no barriers, but you also demand, a truth that is sincere and whole, your soulmate, must truly appreciate, the sublime beauty of living, and participate in your celestial dance.

Your mind is a universe, of ideas that shine like stars, where each thought, is an awakening of new footprints, you are a being of society, who knows how to charm with his talk, and in your dialogue, there are always pearls of wisdom to give away.

Libra, sign of justice, who knows how to measure and consider, your days are a work of art, that you long with passion to color, with brushstrokes of affection, and a desire for unparalleled freedom, towards horizons where the soul can, in its fullness, fly.

Your spirit is a river, that serene and majestic flows without ceasing, in search of eternal beauty, that knows how to venerate with reverence, you are a complex sign, that does not easily let itself be deciphered, and in your deep essence, there is an ocean of mysteries to navigate.

You are the perfect balance, between giving and receiving, the justice you long for, to distribute throughout the world, you are Libra, noble sign, that teaches to build, a bright future, where everyone can share.

Thus, with verses that flow, like the river to the sea, I celebrate you, Libra, in your constant and noble search, for perfect harmony, that teaches us to walk, on the path of life, with justice, love and equity.

And so, like the leaves that write their last verse in the autumn wind, we close the cover of "Libra". Each poem has been a balance that has weighed our joys and sorrows, our triumphs and defeats, with the delicacy of poetic justice.

May this journey through poetry have been for you, dear reader, like finding balance in the embrace of the starry night, a refuge in the immensity of the universe.

May the words here resonate in your soul and accompany you, like the constant search for harmony that defines Libra.

We say goodbye, not as one who ends a chapter, but as one who looks towards the horizon, knowing that balance is an eternal dance between two forces. May the inspiration of "Libra" be the light that guides your steps on the path of life, full of poetry and beauty.

NAMASKARAM

www.ingramcontent.com/pod-product-compliance
Lightning Source LLC
Chambersburg PA
CBHW051841130726
47987CB00002B/638